By Lady Gregory

Irish Folk-History Plays
First Series : The Tragedies
Grania. Kincora. Dervorgilla
Second Series : The Tragic Comedies
The Canavans. The White Cockade. The Deliverer

New Comedies
The Bogie Men. The Full Moon. Coats. Damer's Gold. McDonough's Wife

Our Irish Theatre
A Chapter of Autobiography

Seven Short Plays
Spreading the News. Hyacinth Halvey. The Rising of the Moon. The Jackdaw. The Workhouse Ward. The Travelling Man. The Gaol Gate

Irish Folk-History Plays

By

Lady Gregory

First Series

The Tragedies

Grania—Kincora—Dervorgilla

G. P. Putnam's Sons

New York and London

The Knickerbocker Press

The Knickerbocker Press, New York

THESE THREE PLAYS CONCERNING
STRONG PEOPLE OF THE WORLD I
OFFER TO THEODORE ROOSEVELT
ONE OF THE WORLD'S STRONG MEN

CONTENTS

v

GRANIA

PERSONS
Grania
Finn
Diarmuid
Two Young Men

ACT I

Scene: The scene is laid at Almhuin in Ireland. Time, evening. Inside a richly decorated tent; a fire in brazier centre, a high candlestick at each side; a table with round loaves and wine. An opening at each side of tent. Finn is leading in Grania; she is wearing a golden dress and jewels. Music and joyous shouts are heard outside.

Finn: My five hundred welcomes to you, Grania, coming into Almhuin.

Grania: I thank you, Finn.

Finn: Who would be welcome if it was not the King of Ireland's daughter, that will be my wife to-morrow?

Grania: Your people that were outside and on the road lighted all the district with fires as I came.

Finn: We would have been better prepared if your coming was not so sudden at the last. You did not come too soon, that is a thing that could not happen. But the big house of Almhuin will

3

not be set out fit for you till to-morrow, and it is in the tents of our captains you and your company must be sheltered to-night.

Grania: It was my father, before going to Lochlann, said he must leave me in a husband's care.

Finn: Who would protect you if I would not?

Grania: I am sure of that. Are you not the best of all the world's big men?

Finn: They told me you could have made great marriages, not coming to me?

Grania: My father was for the King of Foreign, but I said I would take my own road.

Finn: He has great riches and a great name.

Grania: I would have been afraid going to him, hearing talk of him as so dark and wild looking, and his shield tusked with the tusks of a boar.

Finn: You were not in dread coming to me, and you so delicate and so cherished?

Grania: I had an old veneration for you, hearing all my lifetime that you are so gentle to women and to dogs and to little children, and you wrestling with the powers of the world and being so hard in war.

Finn: It would be strange any person not to be gentle with you.

Grania: And another thing. I had no wish to go travelling forth and hither to strange countries and by strange seas. I have no mind for going through crosses. I would sooner pass my life at Almhuin, where I ever and always heard there are wide white halls and long tables, and poets and fine company.

Finn: Your father has a good house.

Grania: There was little to listen to but my father planning the wars in Lochlann. There was no pleasant stir in it, unless what there might be in myself.

Finn: It may be you will tire of Almhuin itself after a while.

Grania: There will be good company. I have heard talk of the men and the captains of the Fenians, of Oisin and Osgar and Goll, that came to meet me a while ago.

Finn: The man you will think most of is not with them to-day, that is my own kinsman, Diarmuid.

Grania: I heard of him often. They say him to be the best lover of women in the whole world, and the most daring in the war.

Finn: He has a good name from gentle and simple, from the big man and from the poor. Those even that have no call to him, cannot but love him.

Grania: It was he fought seven days and seven nights with the terrible wild ox upon the mountains.

Finn: Any time I am tired or fretted, all he could do for me he would not think it enough.

Grania: Where is he at this time, that he did not come to meet me with the rest?

Finn: I sent him to a far lonesome hill where I have a secret store of treasures and of jewels. It is right there should be a good man to guard them upon the road. It is for you he is bringing them, he will be here within a short while.

Grania: It is likely it is a man of that sort a woman would find it easy to love.

Finn: Did you ever give a thought to any man in the way of love?

Grania: I did—at least I think I did—but that was a long time ago.

Finn: Who was he? Did he belong to your own place?

Grania: I do not know. I never heard his name—but I saw him.

Finn: Did you speak to him?

Grania: No, he was but as if a shadow, that came for a moment and was gone.

Finn: Tell me all the story.

Grania: They had been hunting—there were a great many strangers. I was bade keep away from the hall. I was looking from a high window —then there was a great outcry in the yard—the hounds were fighting, the hounds the strange men had brought with them. One of them made as if to attack a little dog I owned at the time—I screamed out at the hounds. Then a young man ran out and beat them away, and he held up my little dog to me, laughing, and his cap fell off from his head.

Finn: Did they not tell you his name?

Grania: I was shy to ask them, and I never saw him again. But my thoughts went with him for a good while, and sometimes he came through my dreams.—Is that now what you would call love?

Finn: Indeed, I think it is little at all you know of it.

Grania: I heard often in the stories of people that were in pain and under locks through love. But I think they are but foolishness. There was one of a lover was made go through a fire for his sweetheart's sake, and came out shivering. And one that climbed to his darling's window by one golden thread of her hair.

Finn: There are many such tales and there are more in the making, for it is likely the tearing and vexing of love will be known so long as men are hot-blooded and women have a coaxing way.

Grania: I asked the old people what love was, and they gave me no good news of it at all. Three sharp blasts of the wind they said it was, a white blast of delight and a grey blast of discontent and a third blast of jealousy that is red.

Finn: That red blast is the wickedest of the three.

Grania: I would never think jealousy to be so bad a smart.

Finn: It is a bad thing for whoever knows it. If love is to lie down on a bed of stinging nettles, jealousy is to waken upon a wasp's nest.

Grania: But the old people say more again about love. They say there is no good thing to be gained without hardship and pain, such as a child to be born, or a long day's battle won. And I think it might be a pleasing thing to have a lover that would go through fire for your sake.

Finn: I knew enough of the heat of love in my time, and I am very glad to have done with it now, and to be safe from its torments and its whip and its scourge.

Grania: It being so bad a thing, why, I wonder, do so many go under its sway? That should be a good master that has so many servants and is so well obeyed.

Finn: We do not take it up of ourselves but it sweeps us away before it, and asks no leave. When that blast comes upon us, we are but feathers whirled before it with the dust.

Grania: It is a good thing surely, that I will never know an unhappy, unquiet love, but only love for you that will be by my side for ever. (*A loud peal of laughter is heard outside.*) What is that laughter? There is in it some mocking sound.

Finn: (*Going to the door.*) It is not laughter now—it is a merry outcry as if around some very welcome friend. It is Diarmuid that is come back.

> (*Diarmuid comes in. Grania shrinks back from him.*)

Diarmuid: I am here, Finn, my master.

Finn: What way are you, Diarmuid? There is some wound upon your arm.

Diarmuid: It is a wound I was given on the road. But all you sent me for is safe.

Finn: I knew you would mind them well. But was that hurt cared and eased?

Diarmuid: It is nothing to signify. I drove the robbers off. All is safe. They are bringing the bags in here.

> (*Two fair-haired young men come in two or three times laying bags on floor during the next sentences.*)

I will stop here and mind them through the night time. I would sooner keep charge until you will open them for the wedding on the morrow. I will sit there by the hearth. They are jewels would be coveted by the witches of the lakes, or the sea-women sporting among the golden ribs and the wreckage of the ships of Greece.

Finn: It is to a woman worthy of them they are to be given.

Diarmuid: I am sure of that, indeed, and she being worthy to wed with you.

Finn: Come here, Grania, until I make you acquainted with the branch and the blossom of our young men.

Grania: (*Coming forward.*)   It is—who is it?
        (*She gives a little cry and goes back a step as
            Diarmuid takes off his cap.*)

Finn: What is it ails you, Grania, that you are turned to be so wild and so shy?

Grania: It is that—that—he is wounded.

Finn: You have lost your talk on the road, Diarmuid, you, that were always so ready to string words and praises for comely young women.

Diarmuid: I had no time to wash away the dust and the sweat.   I did not know Grania was in the place.   You should have forewarned me.

Finn: He thinks you are vexed because he is not settled out in handsome clothes.

Grania: It is strange—it is all strange to me— I will get used to meeting strangers.   Another time —in a very short while—my voice will be more steady—my heart will leave starting.

Finn: You will get courage knowing you are a queen.   Where, Diarmuid, is the crown I bade you bring?   It is not the high crown of pearls from the far Indies I want, but the thin golden crown shaped like the rising sun, that I thought of late would be never used, and that I had been keeping till I met with my own queen and my bride.

Diarmuid: It is wrapped about with tanned marten skins and bound with purple thongs.

Finn: (*Unwrapping it.*) Come to me, Grania. (*He puts the crown on her head.*) Courage will come into your heart now, with this sign and token of your estate.

Grania: I am tired. It is weighty on my head —it is time for me to be with myself only. I have seen too much company since morning.

Finn: That is so, and I am much to blame, not taking better thought for you. Come to your women, they will bring you to your tent that is close at hand. You have travelled a long strange road, and to-morrow is your wedding day

Grania: To-morrow? Could it not be put off for a while? This is but May, and no great luck in the moon. There is more luck in the last moon of July—or the first new moon after it. Put it off until that time.

Finn: That cannot be. Your father looked to me to put you in your right place without delay. You must be my wife to-morrow.

Grania: Must it be to-morrow?

Finn: All the armies are gathered together for that, and the feasts are ready. You yourself will be ready when you have taken your sleep through the night time.

Grania: Sleep—sleep—yes, I will go sleep if I can.

Finn: Diarmuid is tired as well as you.

Diarmuid: I have no desire to sleep.   I will sit and watch here till the dawn.

> (*He sits down by the hearth, pulling cloak over his head.   Grania turns back to look at him from the door as Finn takes her out.   After a moment Finn comes back and sits near fire.*)

Finn: Tell me, Diarmuid, is it right that a man past the mering of age should give any thought to love?

Diarmuid: It is right for a man with a great burden of care upon him to have a place of his own where he can let it fall from him.   And what is a home or a house without a wife and a companion at the hearth?

Finn: That is so, and that is what I had in mind at the time this marriage was settled and pressed on, for the good of Ireland and my own good.   But as to love, that is another thing.

Diarmuid: It is another thing, sure enough.

Finn: I thought myself on the far side of it and of its trouble and its joy.   But now this young girl has come to me, so fearless, so mannerly, so plain and simple in her talk, it seems to me I would wed with her, and she not a king's daughter but a poor girl carrying the bag.   (*Diarmuid nods, but is silen'.*)   It is not the one way with you and me, Diarmuid, for many women

have offered you their beauty and themselves;
but as for myself, there is no one I ever gave my
heart to but was swept from me in some hard
way. And this is come like good wine to the
mouth that was filled for a long while with grey
mist and rain. And indeed, indeed my heart
leaps up with her. Is not that natural, Diarmuid,
and she so well reared and so young?

Diarmuid: It is natural, indeed.

Finn: Would you not say her to be well
shaped and of good blood and wise?

Diarmuid: She is all that, indeed.

Finn: It is not often I have known you to be
so begrudging of praise.

Diarmuid: What call have I to be praising
her? I could tell you no more than you knew
before, through your own heart and through your
eyes.

Finn: But, tell me this, now. Is she that is
so airy and beautiful any sort of a fitting wife
for me?

Diarmuid: You are brave and she will put her
pride in you. You are the best of all, and she is
a woman would only join with the best.

Finn: With all that, I would be well pleased
if I could change my years for yours, Diarmuid. I
would give you in their place all the riches I have
ever won.

Diarmuid: Such a woman will be a right head

for Almhuin.   She is used to a king's house, she will be open-handed, and open-hearted along with that.

Finn: I think, indeed, she will be a right wife for me, and loyal.   And it is well that is so, for if ever any man should come between her thoughts and mine I would not leave him living, but would give him the sorrow of death.

Diarmuid: There is no good lover in Ireland but would do the same, and his wife or his sweetheart failing him.

Finn: Yet, in the end there are but few do it; for the thought of men that have passed their midday is mixed with caution and with wisdom and the work they have in hand, or weakness is gaining on their limbs.   And as for youngsters, they do not know how to love, because there is always some to-morrow's love possible in the shadow of the love of to-day.   It is only the old it goes through and through entirely, because they know all the last honey of the summer time has come to its ferment in their cup, and that there is no new summer coming to meet them for ever. And so (*he gets up and stirs fire*) they think to carry that cup through life and death and even beyond the grave.   But can I bring this young girl to be satisfied with that one love?

Diarmuid: There is no one among the men of Ireland can stand against your will.   It should be easy for you to keep a woman faithful.

Finn: Yet the story-tellers make out that love is the disturber; that where it is on the road it is hard to be sure of any woman at all or any friend.

Diarmuid: It is I can give you out an answer to that. My master, you are sure of me.

Finn: I am sure of you, indeed, and it is many a time you put your life in danger for my sake.

Diarmuid: (*Standing up.*) I am your son and your servant always, and your friend. And now, at this marriage time, I will ask one asking.

Finn: Who would get his desire and you not to get it?

Diarmuid: I am tired of courts and of sports and of wars where we gain the day always. I want some hard service to put my hand to. There are the dark men of Foreign, their King has laid it down he will come and master Ireland. Let me go out now and put him down in his own country.

Finn: I will give you leave, but not till after the wedding moon.

Diarmuid: No, but let me go now, this very night, at the brink of dawn.

Finn: No, but stop near me. You are more to me than any of my comrades or my friends.

Diarmuid: It is a strange thing, the first asking I have made, you have refused me.

Finn: Go then and take your own way, and my blessing go with you.

Diarmuid: I thank you for that leave.

Finn: But you will be tired out before morning.   You have been on the road these three days, you got no sleep last night.

Diarmuid: I am drowsy enough and tired, but I will go.

Finn: Lie down over there upon the otter skins. I will sit here by the fire and keep a watch in your place.

Diarmuid: Make a promise then, to wake me at the first whitening of the dawn.

Finn: I will do that.

> (*Diarmuid lies down on skins and sleeps. Finn looks at him a moment and covers him, then puts out candles and sits down where Diarmuid had been sitting, pulling his cloak over his head. Silence a moment, Grania comes in.*)

Grania: (*In a low voice.*) Diarmuid! (*No answer.*) Diarmuid! (*She comes nearer to Finn and speaks a little louder.*) Diarmuid, help me! (*Finn slightly moves.*) Give me your help now. I cannot wed with Finn. I cannot go to him as his wife. I do not know what has happened—half an hour ago I was content to go to him. You came in—I knew you—it was you I saw that day at Tara—my heart started like a deer a while ago. There is something gone astray—the thought of Finn is different. What way could I live beside him and my heart, as I am thinking, gone from him? What name might I be calling out in my sleep? (*She goes close to Finn and puts her hand on his shoulder.*) Have you no way to help me, Diarmuid? It would be a terrible thing, a wedded woman not to be loyal—to call out another man's name in her sleep. (*Finn gets up and goes back into shadow.*) Oh, do not turn away from me! Do not leave me to the marriage I am in dread of. You will not help me? Is it you, Diarmuid, are failing me, you that came to my help that other time. Is it to fail me you will now? And is it my fault if this strange thing has come upon me, and that there is as if no one in all the world but you? You are angry with me and vexed, and it is a bad day, the day I came into this place. But I am not ashamed. Was it my fault at all? I will light now this candle, I will dare to show you my face. You will see in that I am not come to you as a light woman that turns this way and that way, but that I have given you the love I never gave to any man and never will give to any other! (*She lights candle and holds it up.*)

Finn: (*Sternly.*) Grania!

Grania: Oh! It is Finn! And where then is Diarmuid!

Finn: There he is before you. It is the boy

lying down and rising with me has betrayed
me.

Diarmuid: (*Moving and starting up.*) What
is it? What has happened? Is that Grania?

Finn: You were looking for her to come. She
was ready and willing. You are well fitted to
rear traitors to one another.

Diarmuid: You are out of your wits. I
had no thought she was coming here. What
brought her?

Finn: Did she come giving you her love un-
asked? I thought she was a king's daughter.

Diarmuid: She is, and well worthy!

Finn: What was her mother then? Was she
some woman of the camp? (*Pushes her from
him.*)

Diarmuid: (*Putting his arm round her.*) I will
not let any man say that. (*Half draws sword.*)

Finn: My life is a little thing beside what
you have taken!

Diarmuid: You are talking folly. You never
found a lie after me in any sort of way. But
the time courage was put in your heart there
was madness furrowed in your brain!

Finn: Was it every whole minute of your life
you were false to me?

Diarmuid: You would not have said that, the
day I freed you from the three Kings of the Island
of the Floods.

Finn: It is quickly you have been changed by a false woman's flattering words!

Grania: It is not his fault! It is mine! It is on me the blame is entirely! It is best for me to go out a shamed woman. But I will not go knocking at my father's door! I will find some quick way to quiet my heart for ever. Forgive me, Finn, and I have more cause yet to ask you to forgive me, Diarmuid. And if there were hundreds brought together this day for my wedding, it is likely there will be at my burying but the plover and the hares of the bog! (*Goes towards door.*)

Diarmuid: (*Seizing her.*) I will not let you go out this way. I will not fail you!

Finn: There is all your talk of faith to me gone down the wind!

Diarmuid: I will not forsake her, but I will keep my faith with you. I give my word that if I bring her out of this, it is as your queen I will bring her and show respect to her, till such time as your anger will have cooled and that you will let her go her own road. It is not as a wife I will bring her, but I will keep my word to you, Finn.

Finn: Do you give me your oath to that?

Diarmuid: I do give it.

Finn: It is likely it will soon be broken. Grania is no withered pitiful hag with the hair matted wild to her knees.

Diarmuid: It will not be broken. Let my own heart break and be torn by wild dogs before that promise will be broken at all.

Finn: The moon is coming now to the full, and before its lessening you will have lied to me.

Diarmuid: (*Taking up a loaf.*) Look at this cake of bread. I will send you its like, white and round and unbroken at every moon of the year, full moon and harvest moon, while I am along with her, as a sign my own oath is in the same way clean and whole and unbroken.

Finn: It is the woman will make you break that swearing. There will be another telling bye and bye.

Diarmuid: (*Taking Grania's hands.*) There is this league between us, Grania. I will bring you with me and I will keep you safe from every danger. But understand well, it is not as a wife I will bring you, but I will keep my faith with Finn.

Grania: Do as is pleasing to you. I have made an end of askings.

Diarmuid: Come out with me now, till I put you in some place of safety.

Finn: You will find no safety in any place or in any Connacht corner north or west. And out in the big world itself, there is no one will give my enemy so much as shelter from the rain.

Diarmuid: I know well I have earned enemies

in the big world because I fought with all its best men for your sake.

Grania: Oh, take me, take me away out of this! For it is hard treatment is falling upon me!

Diarmuid: And I tell you, Grania, but that I am bound to Finn by my word I have given him, and by kindnesses past counting and out of measure, it would be better to me than the riches of the whole world, you to have given me your love!

Grania: I have given it to you indeed. (*She puts up her face to be kissed.*)

Diarmuid: (*Kissing her forehead.*) That is the first kiss and it will be the last.

Finn: You will give up your life as the charge for that kiss!

Grania: Come out! Come out! The very blood of my heart is rising against him!

Finn: I will not let you go! Let our wedding be here and now, and I will call in as my witnesses to that word Goll and Oisin and Osgar and the captains of the armies of the Fenians!

> (*Finn goes to door, blows horn, then turns towards Grania as if to seize her, sways and falls.*)

Grania Oh, is it death!

Diarmuid: It is but a weakness that took hold of him, with the scorching of his jealousy and its flame.

Grania: Come away before he will rise up and follow us. My father's horses are in the field outside.

Diarmuid: Come out then to the hunting— for it is a long hunting it will be, and it is little comfort we will have from this out. For that is a man driven by anger, and that will not fail from our track so long as the three of us are in the living world!

> (*The sound of many horns and shouts is heard at Right. Diarmuid opens door at Left. Grania goes out quickly. He follows with bowed head.*)

Curtain

Act II

*Scene: Interior of a rough tent. The door opens
on a wood outside. A bed strewn with rushes.
Diarmuid lying on it asleep. Grania is moving
about and singing.*

Grania: Sleep a little, a little little;
Green the wild rushes under my dear.
Sleep here quiet, easy and quiet,
Safe in the wild wood, nothing to fear.
> (*She stirs fire and puts some round cakes she
> has been making, to bake over it. Then
> comes to Diarmuid and puts her hand on
> him as she sings:*)
Waken darling, darling waken!
Wild ducks are flying, daylight is kind;
Whirr of wild wings high in the branches.
Hazel the hound stands snuffing the wind!
Diarmuid: (*Awaking and taking her hand.*)
There is a new light in your eyes—there is a new
blush in your cheeks—there is a new pride stirring

in your thoughts. The white sun of Heaven should be well pleased shining on you. Are you well content, Grania, my wife?

Grania: I am well content indeed with my comrade and my man.

Diarmuid: And did you love me ever and always, Grania?

Grania: Did I not tell you long ago, my heart went down to you the day I looked from the high window, and I in my young youth at Tara.

Diarmuid: It was a long waiting we had for our marriage time.

Grania: It was a long waiting, surely.

Diarmuid: Let us put it out of mind and not be remembering it at all. This last moon has made up for all those seven years.

Grania: It was a troublesome time indeed and a very troublesome life. In all that time we never stopped in any place so long as in the shades and the shelters of this wood.

Diarmuid: It seems to me only one day we have been in it. I would not be sorry in this place, there to be the length of a year in the day.

Grania: The young leaves on the beech trees have unfolded since we came.

Diarmuid: I did not take notice of their growth. Oh, my dear, you are as beautiful as the blossoming of the wild furze on the hill.

Grania: It was not love that brought you to wed me in the end.

Diarmuid: It was, surely, and no other thing. What is there but love can twist a man's life, as sally rods are twisted for a gad?

Grania: No, it was jealousy, jealousy of the King of Foreign, that wild dark man, that broke the hedge between us and levelled the wall.

Diarmuid: (*Starting up.*) Do not bring him back to mind! It was rage that cracked me, when I saw him put his arms about you as if to bring you away.

Grania: Was it my fault? I was but gathering a sheaf of rushes for our two beds, and I saw him coming alongside of the stream to the pool. I knew him by the tusks on his shield and the bristled boar-skin cloak.

Diarmuid: What was it ailed you not to call to me?

Grania: You were far away—you would not have heard me—it is he himself would have heard my call. And I was no way afraid—I hid myself up in the branches of the big red sally by the pool.

Diarmuid: That was a foolish place to go hiding.

Grania: I thought myself safe and well hidden on the branch that goes out over the stream. What way could I know he would stop at that very place, to wash the otter blood from his spear, and the blood from his hands, and the sweat?

Diarmuid: If I had been near, it is his own blood would have splashed away in the pool.

Grania: He stopped then to throw the water on his face—it was my own face he saw in the pool. He looked up of a sudden—he gave a great delighted laugh.

Diarmuid: My lasting grief that I was not there, and my hand gripping his throat.

Grania: He bent the branch—he lifted me from it—he not to have caught me in his arms I would have fallen in the stream.

Diarmuid: That itself might have been better than his hand to have rested on you at all!

Grania: Then you were there—within one minute. You should likely have heard the great shout he gave out and the laugh?

Diarmuid: I lifted my hand to strike at him, and it was as if struck down. It is grief to my heart that he escaped me! I would have crushed him and destroyed him and broken his carcase against the rocks.

Grania: It was I myself struck your hand down. I was well pleased seeing you in that rage of anger.

Diarmuid: If I had known that, it is likely I would have killed you in his place.

Grania: But you did not kill me.

Diarmuid: What was it happened? I was as if blind—you were in my arms not his,—my lips were on the lips he had nearly touched, that I myself had never touched in all those seven years.

Grania: It was a long, long kiss.

Diarmuid: That moment was like the whole of life in a single day, and yet it was but a second of time. And when I looked around he was gone, and there was no trace of him and he had made away and I could not kill him.

Grania: What matter? You should forgive him, seeing it was he brought us together at the last. You should help him to win another kingdom for that good deed. There is nothing will come between us now. You are entirely my own.

Diarmuid: I am belonging to you, indeed, now and for ever. I will bring you away from this rambling life, to a place will be all our own. We will do away with this trade of wandering, we will go on to that bare shore between Burren and the big sea. There will be no trace of our footsteps on the hard flagstones.

Grania: We were in that craggy place before and we were forced to quit it. To live on the wind and on the air you cannot. The wind is not able to support anybody.

Diarmuid: We will get a currach this time.

We will go out over the waves to an island.
The sea and the strand are wholesome. We
shall sleep well, and the tide beating its watch
around us.

Grania: Even out in those far Aran Islands
we would be threatened and driven as happened
in the time past.

Diarmuid: But beyond Aran, far out in the
west, there is another island that is seen but
once in every seven years.

Grania: Is that a real place at all? Or is it
only in the nurses' tales?

Diarmuid: Who knows? There is no good
lover but has seen it at some time through his
sleep. It is hid under a light mist, away from
the track of traders and kings and robbers. The
harbour is well fenced to keep out loud creak-
ing ships. Some fisherman to break through the
mist at some time, he will bring back news
of a place where there is better love and a better
life than in any lovely corner of the world that
is known. (*She turns away.*) And will you
come there with me, Grania?

Grania: I am willing to go from this.
We cannot stop always in the darkness of
the woods— but I am thinking it should be
very strange there and very lonesome.

Diarmuid: The sea-women will rise up giving
out news of the Country-under-Wave, and

the birds will have talk as in the old days. And maybe some that are beyond the world will come to keep us company, seeing we are fitted to be among them by our unchanging love.

Grania: We are going a long time without seeing any of the people of the world, unless it might be herds and fowlers, and robbers that are hiding in the wood.

Diarmuid: It is enough for us having one another. I would sooner be talking with you than with the world wide.

Grania: It is likely some day you will be craving to be back with the Fenians.

Diarmuid: I was fretting after them for a while. But now they are slipping out of mind. It would seem as if some soul-brothers of my own were calling to me from outside the world. It may be they have need of my strength to help them in their hurling and their wars.

Grania: I have not had the full of my life yet, for it is scared and hiding I have spent the best of my years that are past. And no one coming to give us news or knowledge, and no friendly thing at all at hand, unless it might be Hazel the hound, or that I might throw out a handful of meal to the birds to bring me company. I would wish to bring you back now to some busy peopled place.

Diarmuid: You never asked to be brought to such a place in all our time upon the road. And are you not better pleased now than when we dragged lonely-hearted and sore-footed through the days?

Grania: I am better pleased, surely—and it is by reason of that I would wish my happiness to be seen, and not to be hidden under the branches and twigs of trees.

Diarmuid: If I am content here, why would not you be content?

Grania: It is time for you to have attendance again, and good company about you. We are the same here as if settled in the clay, clogged with the body and providing for its hunger and its needs, and the readying of the dinner of to-day and the providing of the dinner for to-morrow. It is at the head of long tables we should be, listening to the old men with their jokes and flatteries, and the young men making their plans that will change the entire world.

Diarmuid: That is all over for me now, and cast away like the husk from the nut.

Grania: They will be forgetting us altogether.

Diarmuid: No, but they will put us into songs, till the world will wonder at the luck of those two lovers that carried love entire and unbroken out beyond the rim of sight.

Grania: That may be. And some night at

the supper the men will turn their heads
hearing that song and will say, "Is Diarmuid
living yet?" or "Grania must be withered now
and a great trouble to those that are about
her." And they will turn to the women that
are smiling beside them, and that have delicate
hands, and little blushes in their cheeks, and that
are maybe but my own age all the same, but
have kept their young looks, being merry and well
cared. And Grania and Diarmuid will be no
more than a memory and a name.

Diarmuid: (*Taking her hand.*) These white
hands were always willing hands, and where,
I wonder, was this discontent born? A little
while ago it was the woods you wanted, and
now it is the palaces you want.

Grania: It is not my mind that changes, it
is life that changes about me. If I was content
to be in hiding a while ago, now I am proud and
have a right to be proud. And it is hard to
nourish pride in a house having two in it only.

Diarmuid: I take pride in you here, the same
as I would in any other place.

Grania: Listen to me. You are driving me
to excuses and to words that are not entirely
true. But here, now, is truth for you. All the
years we were with ourselves only, you kept
apart from me as if I was a shadow-shape or a
hag of the valley. And it was not till you saw

another man craving my love, that the like love was born in yourself. And I will go no more wearing out my time in lonely places, where the martens and hares and badgers run from my path, but it is to thronged places I will go, where it is not through the eyes of wild startled beasts you will be looking at me, but through the eyes of kings' sons that will be saying: "It is no wonder Diarmuid to have gone through his crosses for such a wife!" And I will overhear their sweethearts saying: "I would give the riches of the world, Diarmuid to be my own comrade." And our love will be kept kindled for ever, that would be spent and consumed in desolate places, like the rushlight in a cabin by the bog. (For it is certain it is by the respect of others we partly judge even those we know through and through.)

Diarmuid: (*Getting up and speaking gravely.*) There is no going back for us, Grania, and you know that well yourself.

Grania: We will go to my father's house— he is grown old, he will not refuse me—we will call to your people and to my people—we will bring together an army of our own.

Diarmuid: That is enough of arguing. There is no sense or no reason in what you are saying.

Grania: It is a bad time you have chosen to give up your mannerly ways. You did not speak that way the day you found me in the hand of the King of Foreign. You would maybe be better pleased if I had gone with him at that time.

Diarmuid: You are but saying that to vex and to annoy me. You are talking like an innocent or a fool.

Grania: He made me great promises. A great place and power and great riches.

Diarmuid: I can win you riches in plenty if that is what you are coveting in your mind.

Grania: I cared little for his talk of riches— but—when he put his arms about me and kissed me——

Diarmuid: You let him leave a kiss upon your mouth?

Grania: It as if frightened me—it seemed strange to me—there came as if a trembling in my limbs. I said: "I am this long time going with the third best man of the Fenians, and he never came as near as that to me."

Diarmuid: (*Flinging her from him.*) Go then your own way, and I would be well pleased never to have met you, and I was no better than a fool, thinking any woman at all could give love would last longer than the froth upon the stream!

(*The sound of a rattle is heard outside.*)
Grania: What is that? Who is it?

3

(Finn disguised as a beggar is seen at door.)

Diarmuid: It is but a beggar or a leper.

Finn: Is this a house is sheltering a handsome young woman and a lathy tall young man, that are not belonging to this district, and having no follower but a hound?

Diarmuid: Who are you? Keep back from the door!

Finn: I am no leper if I am a beggar. And my name is well earned that is Half-Man—for there is left to me but one arm by the wolves, and one side of my face by the crows that came picking at me on the ridge where I was left for dead. And beyond that again, one of the feet rotted from me, where I got it hurted one time through a wound was given me by treachery in the heel.

Diarmuid: Take off that mask till I see your face.

Finn: I will and welcome, if you have a mind to see it, but it is not right a lovely young lady to get a view of a bare gnawed skull, and that is what this caul covers. It is by reason of that I go sounding the rattle, to scare children from the path before me, and women carrying child.

Diarmuid: If it is alms you are seeking it is a bare place to come, for we carry neither gold or silver, there being no market in the woods.

Finn: Not at all, not at all—I am asking nothing at all. Believe me, the man that sent me is a good payer of wages.

Diarmuid: What call had he to send you here? We own nothing for any man to covet.

Finn: With a message he sent me, a message. You to be the man and the young woman I am searching after, I have to give a message and get a message. That is all the business I have to do. I will get fair play, never fear, from the man that sent me.

Diarmuid: Tell me who is that man, till I know is he enemy or friend.

Finn: You to see him you would not forget him. A man he is, giving out gold from his hand the same as withered leaves, and having on his shield the likeness of the rising sun.

Grania: That can surely be no other than Finn. What did he want sending you?

Finn: I will tell you that, and it is little I know why would he want it. You would not say him to be a man would be in need of bread.

Grania: Tell out now what you have to tell.

Finn: Would n't you say it to be a strange thing, a man having that much gold in his hand, and the sun in gold on his shield, to be as hungry after bread as a strayed cur dog would have nothing to eat or to fall back on, and would be yelping after his meal.

Diarmuid: Give out the message.

Finn: It is what he bade me say: "Tell that young woman," he said, "and that youngster with her," he said, "that on every first night of the round moon these seven years, there used to be a round cake of bread laid upon my road. And the moon was at her strength yesterday," he said, "and it has failed me to find on any path that cake of bread."

Diarmuid: It is Finn that sent him! It is Finn is calling me to account because I have forgotten my promise to him, and my faith.

Grania: He has come upon our track. We must go our road again. It is often we escaped him before this. I am no way afraid.

Diarmuid: It is not fear that is on me, it is shame. Shame because Finn thought me a man would hold to my word, and I have not held to it. I am as if torn and broken with the thought and the memory of Finn.

Grania: It is time to put away that memory. It is long enough you gave in to his orders.

Diarmuid: I did that with my own consent. Nothing he put upon me was hard. He trusted me and he could trust me, and now he will never put trust in me again.

Grania: It may not be Finn will be getting his commands done, and our friends gathering to our help. Let him learn that time, not to thrust his hand between the wedges and the splint.

Finn: (*Who has been sitting crouched over fire.*) Have you the message ready and the bread I was bade bring back to the champion that met me on the path?

Grania: (*Taking up one of the cakes.*) It is best send it to him and gain the time to make our escape.

Diarmuid: No, no more lying. I will tell no more lies to my master and my friend!

(*Diarmuid takes cake from Grania and flings it down, then throws himself on the bed and covers his face with his hands. Grania takes up cake, breaks it again and again, and gives it to Finn.*)

Grania: That is the answer to his message. Say to him that as that bread is broken and torn, so is the promise given by the man that did right in breaking it. Tell Finn, the time you meet him, it was the woman herself gave that to you, and bade you leave it in his hand as a message and as a sign!

Finn: Take care now. Is that a right message you are sending, and one that you will not repent?

Grania: It is a right message for that man to get. And give heed to what I say now. If you have one eye is blind, let it be turned to the place where we are, and that he might ask news of. And if you have one seeing eye, cast it upon me, and tell Finn you saw a woman no way sad or afraid, but as airy and high-minded as a mountain filly would be challenging the winds of March!

Finn: I can tell him that, surely, and you not giving it out to me at all.

Grania: And another thing. Tell him there is no woman but would be proud, and that oath being broken for her sake. And tell him she is better pleased than if she was a queen of the queens of the world, that she, a travelling woman going out under the weather, can turn her back on him this day as she did in the time that is past. Go now, and give that message if you dare to give it, and keep those words red scorched in your mind.

Finn: I will bring that message, sure enough, and there will be no fear on me giving it out. For all the world knows Finn never took revenge on a fool, or a messenger, or a hound. But it would be well for them that send it to bear in mind that he is a hard man—a hard man—a hard man, surely. As hard as a barren step-mother's slap, or a highway gander's gob.

Grania: Go, go on your road. Or will you take food and drink before you go?

Finn: Not at all, I will eat in no man's house

or in any place at all, unless in the bats' feeding
time and the owls', the way the terror of my face
will not be seen. I will be going now, going my
road. But, let you mind yourself. Finn does be
very wicked the time he does be mad vexed. And
he is a man well used to get the mastery, and any
that think to go daring him, or to go against him,
he will make split marrow of their bones.

Diarmuid: (*Looking up.*) There might kindness grow in him yet. It is not big men, the
like of him, keep up enmity and a grudge for
ever.

Finn: Who can know, who can know? Finn
has a long memory. There is Grania he doted
down on, and that was robbed from him, and
he never threw an eye on any woman since and
never will, but going as if crazed, and ransacking
the whole country after her. As restless as the
moon of Heaven he is, and at some times as
wasted and as pale.

Grania: It is time for him to leave thinking
about her.

Finn: A great memory he has and great
patience, and a strong fit of the jealous, that
is the worst thing ever came from the skies.
How well he never forgave and never will forgive
Diarmuid O'Duibhne, that he reared on his knee
and nourished with every marrow-bone, and that
stole away his wife from him, and is dead.

Grania: That is no true story. Diarmuid is not dead, but living!

Finn; That's my hearing of the thing. And if he is on the earth yet, what is he doing? Would you call that living? Screening himself behind bushes, running before the rustling of a wren on the nest. In dread to face his master or the old companions that he had.

Grania: There is no man but must go through trouble at some time; and many a good man has been a stranger and an exile through a great share of his lifetime.

Finn: I am no friend to Diarmuid O'Duibhne. But he to be my friend, I would think it a great slur upon him it being said a man that had so great a name was satisfied and content, killing hares and conies for the supper, casting at cranes for sport, or for feathers to stuff a pillow for his sweetheart's head, the time there is an army of the men of Foreign in Ireland.

Grania: I can tell you it will not be long till he will be seen going out against them, and going against some that are not foreign, and he having an army of his own.

Finn: It is best for him make no delay so, where they are doing every whole thing to drag the country down.

Diarmuid: (*Standing up.*) I will go out and fight. I will delay no minute.

Grania: No, but do as I tell you. Gather your friends till you can make your own stand. Where is the use of one man only, however good he may be?

Finn: A queer thing indeed, no queerer. Diarmuid, that was the third best man of the whole of the armies of the Fenians, to be plucking and sorting pigeon's feathers to settle out a pillow and a bed.

Diarmuid: I will go as I am, by myself. There is no man living would let his name lie under reproach as my name is under it.

Grania: (*To Finn.*) Go quick—you have brought messages—bring another message for me, now, to the High King's house at Tara.

Diarmuid: I will wait for no man's help. I will go.

Grania: Is it that you will leave me? It is certain Finn has tracked us—we have stopped too long in the one place. If Finn is there his strength will be there. Do not leave me here alone to the power and the treachery of Finn! It is in at this door he may be coming before the fall of night.

Diarmuid: I will stop here. I will not leave you under Finn's power for any satisfaction to myself. (*To Finn.*) Go, as you are bidden, and bring help from the King at Tara.

Finn: Very good, very good. That now is the message of a wise housekeeping husband.

Diarmuid: I give my word it needs more courage at some times to be careful than to be forward and daring, and that is the way with me now.

Finn: Maybe so, maybe so. And there is no wonder at all a common man to be tame and timid, when Diarmuid, grandson of Duibhne has a faint miserable heart.

Diarmuid: That is the wicked lie of some old enemy.

Finn: (*Going to door.*) Very likely, very likely; but maybe it would be better for Grania I was speaking of, to have stopped with the old man that made much of her, in place of going with the young man that belittles her.

Grania: That is a slander and no true word.

Finn: (*At door.*) Ha! Ha! Ha! It is a story makes great sport among gentle and simple in every place. It is great laughing is given out when the story is heard, that the King of Foreign put his arms about Grania's neck that is as white as a hound's tooth, and that Diarmuid saw him do it—and that the King of Foreign is living yet, and goes boasting on his road! (*Goes out.*)

Diarmuid: (*Fastening on sword.*) Give that to me. (*Points at spear.*)

Grania: (*Throwing it from her.*) Oh, stop with me, my darling, and my love, do not go from me now or forsake me! And to stay in the lonely

woods for ever or in any far desolate place, you
will never hear a cross word or an angry word
from me again. And it is for you I will wear my
jewels and my golden dress. For you are my
share of life, and you are the east and the west
to me, and all the long ago and all that is
before me! And there is nothing will come between us or part us, and there will be no name
but yours upon my lips, and no name but my
own spoken by your lips, and the two of us well
contented for ever!

Finn: (*Comes back and looks in at door.*) It
is what they were saying a while ago, the King
of Foreign is grunting and sighing, grunting and
sighing, around and about the big red sally tree
beside the stream! (*He disappears. Diarmuid
rushes out.*)

Curtain

Act III

Scene: In the same tent. Grania has put on her golden dress and jewels, and is plaiting gold into her hair. Horns and music suddenly heard, not very near. She goes startled to door, and falls back as Finn comes in. He is dressed as if for war and has his banner in his hand. He looks older and more worn than in the First Act.

Finn: I have overtaken you at last, Grania.

Grania: Finn! It is Finn! (*She goes a step back and takes up a spear.*)

Finn: It would be no great load upon you to bid me welcome.

Grania: What is it has brought you here?

Finn: Foolishness brought me here, and nature.

Grania: It is foolishness for a man not to stop and mind his own estate.

Finn: A wild bird of a hawk I had, that went

44

out of my hand. I am entitled to it by honest law.

Grania: I know your meaning well. But hearken now and put yourself in a better mind. It is a heavy punishment you put upon us these many years, and it is short till we 'll all be in the grave, and it is as good for you leave us to go our own road.

Finn: A queer long way I would have walked for no profit. Diarmuid is gone out from you. There is nothing to hinder me from bringing you away.

Grania: There is such a thing.

Finn: Is it your own weak hand on that spear?

Grania: (*Throwing it down.*) No, but your own pride, if it has not gone from you and left you snapping and angry, like any moon-crazed dog.

Finn: If there is madness within me, it is you yourself have a right to answer for it. But for all that, it is truth you are speaking, and I will not bring you away, without you will come with me of your own will.

Grania: That will be when the rivers run backward.

Finn: No, but when the tide is at the turn. I tell you, my love that was allotted and foreshadowed before the making of the world will drag you in spite of yourself, as the moon above drags the waves, and they grumbling through the pebbles as they come, and making their own little moaning of discontent.

Grania: You have failed up to this to drag or to lead me to you.

Finn: There is great space for rememberings and regrettings in the days and the nights of seven years.

Grania: I and Diarmuid stopped close to one another all that time, and being as we were without hearth or frolic, or welcome or the faces of friends.

Finn: Many a day goes by, and nothing has happened in it worth while. And then there comes a day that is as if the ring of life, and that holds all the joy and the pain of life between its two darknesses. And I am thinking that day has come, and that it will put you on the road to myself and Almhuin.

Grania: You think I will give in to you because I am poor in the world. But there is grief in my heart I not to have strength to drive that spear through you, and be quit of your talk forever.

Finn: Would you think better of me if I had been satisfied to put this crown on some other woman's head, and it having rested upon your own for one moment of time? (*Takes crown from under his cloak and holds it up.*)

Grania: It would have been best. I would be well pleased to see you do it yet.

Finn: But I would not do that to gain the whole world entirely. And I to have my youth seven times over, it is after you I would come searching those seven times. And I have my life spent and wasted following you, and I have kissed the sign of your foot in every place all through Ireland.

Grania: I have no forgiveness for you that have been a red enemy to my darling and my man. I have too long a memory of all the unkindness you have done.

Finn: It is your fault if I did them. Every time the thought of kindness came to me, the thought of you came with it, and put like a ring of iron around my heart.

Grania: It is turned to iron indeed. And listen to me now, Finn, and believe what I say. You to have hunted us through crags and bushes, and sent us out in the height of hailstones and of rain, I might overlook it and give you pardon. But it is the malice you showed, putting a hedge between myself and Diarmuid that I never will forgive, but will keep it against you for ever. For it is you left my life barren, and it was you came between us two through all the years.

Finn: I did right doing that. There is no

man but would keep the woman he is to wed
for himself only.

Grania: It was your shadow was between us
through all that time, and if I carry hatred
towards you, I leave it on your own head. And
it is little I would have thought of hardships,
and we two being lovers and alone. But that
is not the way it was. For the time he would
come in, sweaty and sorefooted from the hunting,
or would be dull and drowsy from the nights of
watching at the door, I would be down-hearted
and crabbed maybe; or if I was kind itself, it
would be like a woman would be humouring a
youngster, and her mind on some other track.
But we to have a settled home and children
to be fondling, that would not have been the
way with us, and the day would have been
short, and we showing them off to one another,
and laying down there was no one worthy to
have called them into the world but only our
two selves.

Finn: You are saying what is not true, and
what you have no right to say. For you know
well and you cannot deny it, you are man and
wife to one another this day.

Grania: And if we are, it is not the same as
a marriage on that day we left Almhuin would
have been. It was you put him under a promise
and a bond that was against nature, and he was

a fool to make it, and a worse fool to keep it.
And what are any words at all put against the
love of a young woman and a young man? It was
you turned my life to weariness, and my heart
to bitterness, and put me under the laughter
and the scorn of all. For there was not a poor
man's house where we lodged, but I could see
wonder and mockery and pity in the eyes of the
woman of the house, where she saw that poor
as she was, and ugly maybe and ragged, a king's
daughter was thought less of than herself. Because if Diarmuid never left his watch upon my
threshold, he never came across it, or never gave
me the joy and pride of a wife! And it was
you did that on me, and I leave it on your own
head; and if there is any hatred to be found in
the world, and it to be squeezed into one cup
only, it would not be so black and so bitter as
my own hatred for you!

Finn: That hatred is as if crushed out of the
great bulk of my love for you, that is heaped
from the earth to the skies.

Grania: I am not asking it or in need of it.
Why would I listen to a story I have heard often
and too often.

Finn: But you will listen, and you will give
heed to it. You came of your own free will to
Almhuin to be my wife. And my heart went
out to you there and then, and I thought there

4

would be the one house between us, and that
it was my child I would see reared on your knee.
And that was known to every one of my people
and of my armies, and you were willing it should
be known. And after that, was it a little thing
that all Ireland could laugh at the story that I,
Finn, was so spent, and withered, and loathsome
in a woman's eyes, that she would not stop with
me in a life that was full and easy, but ran out
from me to travel the roads, the same as any
beggar having seven bags. And I am not like
a man of the mean people, that can hide his grief
and his heart-break, bringing it to some district
where he is not known, but I must live under that
wrong and that insult in full sight of all, and
among mockery and malicious whisperings in the
mouth of those maybe that are shouting me!

Grania: I have a great wrong done to you,
surely, but it brings me no nearer to you now.
And our life is settled, and let us each go our
own course.

Finn: Is it not a great wonder the candle you
lighted not to have been quenched in all that time?
But the light in your grey eyes is my desire for
ever, and I am pulled here and there over hills
and through hollows. For my life was as if cut
in two halves on that night that put me to and
fro; and the half that was full and flowing was
put behind me, and it has been all on the ebb

since then. But you and I together could have
changed the world entirely, and put a curb upon
the spring-tide, and bound the seven elements
with our strength. And now, that is not the way
I am, but dragging there and hither, my feet
wounded with thorns, the tracks of tears down
my cheeks; not taking rest on the brink of any
thick wood, because you yourself might be in it,
and not stopping on the near side of any lake or
inver because you might be on the far side; as
wakeful as a herd in lambing time, my companions stealing away from me, being tired with
the one corn-crake cry upon my lips always, that
is, Grania. And it is no wonder the people to
hate you, and but for dread of me they would
many a time have killed you.

Grania: If I did you wrong, did I do no
wrong against Diarmuid? And all the time we
were together he never cast it up against me
that it was I brought him away from his comrades, or, as he could have done, that I asked
him without waiting for his asking. He never
put reproaches on me, as you are reproaching
me, now that I am alone and without any friend
at hand.

Finn: Diarmuid has no harm in his heart, and
he would find it hard to do anything was not
mannerly, and befitting a man reared in king's
houses, if he is no good lover itself.

Grania: Diarmuid that gave all up for love is the best lover of the whole world.

Finn: No, for his love is not worth a reed of straw beside mine.

Grania: His love knows no weakening at all. He would begrudge me to walk the road! Listen to this now. The King of Foreign had put his arms about me—he had left but one kiss on my mouth—and for that much Diarmuid is gone out at this time to take his life!

Finn: Diarmuid to be a good lover, it is my own life he would have shortened. If he had any great love for you, it is I myself he would not have left living.

Grania: You are belittling Diarmuid, and I will judge you by your own words. You boast that you are a better lover. Then why are you wasting talk here, and you having let him go out of your hand to-day?

Finn: He is not gone out of reach of my hand.

Grania: He is! He is safe and gone from you. Would I have been so daring in talk, and I not certain of that?

Finn: It is hard for any man to escape the thing was laid down for him, and that he has earned.

Grania: It is no friend of yours he went out fighting. It is that foreign king. He will be well able to put him down.

Finn: It is not a man weakened with love that goes out to win in a fight. It is a foreign hand will do judgment upon him, but it was I myself sent him out to that judgment.

Grania: That is not true! It is a boast and a bragging you are making to threaten me. You would never dare to do it. He is of your own blood.

Finn: You are beautiful and I am old and scarred. But if it was different, and I to be what I was, straight as a flag-flower, and yellow-haired, and you what the common people call out that hate you, wide and low-born, a hedgehog, an ugly thing, I would kill any man at all that would come between us, because you are my share of the world and because I love you.

Grania: You are speaking lies—I know it is a lie and that it was not you sent him out to that fight. It was not you, it was that sharp-tongued beggar, that spiteful crippled man.

Finn: There is no man only a lover, can be a beggar, and not ashamed.

Grania: It was not you—you were not that cripple.

Finn: This is the hand where you put the broken bread.

Grania: It was you sent Diarmuid out! It was you came between us! It was you parted us! It was your voice he obeyed and listened to, the time he had no ears for me! Are you between us always?—I will go out after him, I will call him back—I will tell him your treachery—he will make an end of it and of you. He will know you through and through this time. It will fail you to come between us again.

(*A heavy shout is heard.*)

Finn: Hush, and listen! (*Goes to the door.*)

Grania: What is it? Let me find Diarmuid——

Finn: (*Holding her back.*) It is Diarmuid is coming in.

> (*Diarmuid's body is carried in by two fair-haired young men. They lay it on the bed and take off their caps. Finn looks at him, takes his hand, then lays it down and turns away.*)

Death and the judgment of death have over-taken him.

Grania: (*Bending over him.*) Oh, Diarmuid, you are not dead! You cannot be dead! It is not in this hour you could die, and all well between us, and all done away with that had parted us!

Finn: He is dead indeed. Look at that wound in his neck. He is bleeding and destroyed with blood.

Grania: Come back to me, come back, my heart's darling, my one love of the men of the world! Come back, if but for one moment of

time. Come back, and listen to all I have to
tell. And it is well we have the world earned,
and is it not a hard thing, a young man to die
because of any woman at all casting an eye on
him, and making him her choice, and bringing
her own bad luck upon him, that was marked
down for her maybe in the time before the world.
And it is hunger I gave you through my love, and
it is a pity it is around you it was cast, and it is
a pity now, you to be loosed out of it. And it
would have been better for you, some girl of
the ducks and ashes, hard reared and rough, to
have settled out your pillow, and not myself that
brought ill-will upon you, and the readying of
your grave!

Finn: Where is the use of calling to him and
making an outcry? He can hear no word at all,
or understand anything you say. And he has
brought with him a good memory of happiness and
of love; and some of the world's great men bringing with them but empty thoughts of a life that
was blasted and barren.

Grania: Ochone, my grief! For all is at an end,
and you are clean wheat ground and bruised and
broken between two hard stones, the luckless love
of a woman, and the love turned to anger of a
friend.

Finn: (*Putting his hand on her arm.*) That is
enough. A red death is a clean death, and the

thing that is done cannot be undone, and the story is ended, and there is no other word to say.

Grania: (*Pushing him away.*) You stood between us long enough and he living, but you cannot come between us and he dead! And I own him from this time any way, and I am glad and could nearly laugh, knowing your power is spent and run out, and that it will fail you to come meddling any more between us that are lovers now to the end!

Finn: Your bitter words are no matter. There is no one to give heed to them.

Grania: It is well I will keen him, and I never will quit his grave till such time as the one flagstone will cover the two of us from the envious eyes of the women of Ireland and from your own. And a woman to lose her comrade, she loses with him her crown! And let you go to some other place, Finn, for you have nothing to say to him at all, and no other hand will be laid on him from this out but my own!

Finn: (*Bending over him.*) He is not dead—his lips are stirring—there is a little blush in his face——

Grania: (*Stooping.*) Oh, Diarmuid, are you come back to me? (*He moves.*) Speak to me now. Lift now your lips to my own—hush! He is going to speak. Oh, Diarmuid, my darling, give me one word!

Diarmuid: (*Turns his head slightly and looks at Finn.*) Is that you, my master, Finn? I did not know you were dead along with me.

Grania: You are not dead, you are living—my arms are about you. This is my kiss upon your cheek. (*Kisses him.*)

Diarmuid: (*Not noticing her.*) The King of Foreign is dead. I struck him down by the sally tree—as he was falling he struck at me, and the life went out of me. But what way did you meet with your death, my master Finn?

Grania: You are living I say—turn towards me. I am Grania, your wife.

Diarmuid: (*Still speaking to Finn.*) It is a very friendly thing you to have met me here, and it is Ireland and the world should be lonesome after you this day!

Grania: Speak to him, Finn. Tell him he is astray. Tell him he is living. Bring the wits back to him.

Finn: Diarmuid, you are not dead, you are in the living world.

Grania: Come back, now, come back to life! Finn thought he had sent you to your death, but it failed him—he is treacherous—he is no friend to you. You will know that now. Come back, and leave thinking of him!

Diarmuid: (*Still speaking to Finn.*) There

was some word I had to say meeting you—it is gone—I had it in my mind a while ago.

Grania: Do you not see me? It is I myself am here—Grania!

Diarmuid: Some wrong I did you, some thing past forgiving. Is it to forgive me you are waiting here for me, and to tell me you are keeping no anger against me after all?

Finn: Come back now, and put out your strength, and take a good grip of life, and I will give you full forgiveness for all you have done against me. And I will have done with anger, and with jealousy that has been my bedfellow this long time, and I will meddle with you no more, unless in the way of kindness.

Diarmuid: Kindness—you were always kind surely, and I a little lad at your knee. Who at all would be kind to me and you not being kind?

Finn: I will turn back altogether, I will leave you Grania your wife, and all that might come between us from this time.

Diarmuid: What could there be would come between us two? That would be a strange thing indeed.

Finn: I will go, for the madness is as if gone from me; and you are my son and my darling, and it is beyond the power of any woman to put us asunder, or to turn you against me any more.

Diarmuid: That would be a very foolish man

would give up his dear master and his friend for any woman at all. (*He laughs.*)

Grania: He is laughing—the sense is maybe coming back to him.

Diarmuid: It would be a very foolish thing, any woman at all to have leave to come between yourself and myself. I cannot but laugh at that.

Finn: Rouse yourself up now, and show kindness to the wife that is there at your side.

Diarmuid: There is some noise of the stream where I died. It is in my ears yet—but I remember—I am remembering now—there was something I begrudged you, the time our bodies were heavy about us. Something I brought away from you, and kept from you. What wildness came upon me to make me begrudge it? What was it I brought away from you? Was not Hazel my own hound? (*He dies.*)

Finn: Lift up your head, open your eyes, do not die from me! Come back to me, Diarmuid, now!

Grania: He will say no word to either one of us again for ever. (*She goes to wall, leaning her head against it, her hands working.*)

Finn: Are you gone indeed, Diarmuid, that I myself sent to your death? And I would be well pleased it was I, Finn, was this day making clay, and you yourself holding up your head among the armies. It is a bad story for me you to be dead, and it is in your place I would be

well satisfied to be this day; and you had not
lived out your time. But as to me, I am tired
of all around me, and all the weight of the years is
come upon me, and there will be no more joy in
anything happens from this day out forever.
And it is as if all the friends ever I had went to
nothing, losing you. (*After a moment's silence
he turns to the young men.*) Bring him out now,
slaves of Britain, to his comrades and his friends,
and the armies that are gathering outside, till
they will wake him and mourn him and give him
burial, for it is a king is lost from them this day.
And if you have no mind to keen him, let you
raise a keen for the men of your own country he
left dumb in the dust, and a foolish smile on their
face. For he was a good man to put down his
enemies and the enemies of Ireland, and it is living
he would be this day if it was not for his great
comeliness and the way he had, that sent every
woman stammering after him and coveting him;
and it was love of a woman brought him down in
the end, and sent him astray in the world. And
what at all is love, but lies on the lips and drunk-
enness, and a bad companion on the road?

> (*The body is carried out. The bearers begin to
> keen. The keen is taken up by the armies
> outside. Finn sits down, his head bowed
> in his hand. Grania begins fastening up
> her hair and as if preparing for a journey.*

Finn: You are doing well going out to keen after him.

Grania: It is not with him I am going. It is not with Diarmuid I am going out. It is an empty thing to be crying the loss of a comrade that banished me from his thoughts, for the sake of any friend at all. It is with you I will go to Almhuin. Diarmuid is no more to me than a sod that has been quenched with the rain.

Finn: I will meddle no more with what belongs to him. You are the dead man's wife.

Grania: All the wide earth to come between Diarmuid and myself, it would put us no farther away from one another than what we are. And as for the love I had for him, it is dead now, and turned to be as cold as the snow is out beyond the path of the sun.

Finn: It is the trouble of the day that is preying on you.

Grania: He had no love for me at any time. It is easy know it now. I knew it all the while, but I would not give in to believe it. His desire was all the time with you yourself and Almhuin. He let on to be taken up with me, and it was but letting on. Why would I fret after him that so soon forgot his wife, and left her in a wretched way?

Finn: You are not judging him right. You are distracted with the weight of your loss.

Grania: Does any man at all speak lies at the very brink of death, or hold any secret in his heart? It was at that time he had done with deceit, and he showed where his thought was, and had no word at all for me that had left the whole world for his sake, and that went wearing out my youth, pushing here and there as far as the course of the stars of Heaven. And my thousand curses upon death not to have taken him at daybreak, and I believing his words! It is then I would have waked him well, and would have cried my seven generations after him! And I have lost all on this side of the world, losing that trust and faith I had, and finding him to think of me no more than of a flock of stairs would cast their shadow on his path. And I to die with this scald upon my heart, it is hard thistles would spring up out of my grave.

Finn: Quiet yourself, for this is grief gone wild and that is beyond all measure.

Grania: I to have known that much yesterday I would have left him and would have gone with that King that clutched at me. And I would have said words to Diarmuid would have left a burn and a sting.

Finn: I will call in women to cry with you and to be comforting you.

Grania: You are craving to get rid of me

now, and to put me away out of your thoughts,
the same as Diarmuid did. But I will not
go! I will hold you to your word, I will take
my revenge on him! He will think to keep
your mind filled with himself and to keep me
from you,—he will be coming back showing himself as a ghost about Almhuin. He will think
to come whispering to you, and you alone in
the night time. But he will find me there before
him! He will shrink away lonesome and baffled!
I will have my turn that time. It is I will
be between him and yourself, and will keep
him outside of that lodging for ever!

Finn: I gave him my promise I would leave
you to him from this out, and I will keep
it to him dead, the same as if he was still living.

Grania: How well he kept his own promise to
you! I will go to Almhuin in spite of you;
you will be ashamed to turn me back in the
sight of the people, and they having seen your
feet grown hard in following and chasing me
through the years. It is women are said to
change, and they do not, but it is men that change
and turn as often as the wheel of the moon.
You filled all Ireland with your outcry wanting me, and now, when I am come into your
hand, your love is rusted and worn out. It
is a pity I that had two men, and three men,
killing one another for me an hour ago, to be

left as I am, and no one having any use for me at all!

Finn: It is the hardness of trouble is about my heart, and is bringing me down with its weight. And it seems to me to be left alone with December and the bareness of the boughs; and the fret will be on me to the end.

Grania: Is it not a strange thing, you, that saw the scores and the hundreds stretched dead, that at the sight of one young man only, you give in to the drowning of age. It is little I will give heed from this out to words or to coaxings, and I have no love to give to any man for ever. But Diarmuid that belittled me will not see me beating my hands beside his grave, showing off to the cranes in the willows, and twisting a mournful cry. It is the thing I will give him to take notice of, a woman that cared nothing at all for his treachery.

Finn: Wait till the months of mourning are at an end, and till your big passion is cold, and do then what you may think fit, and settle out your life, as it is likely there will be another thought in your mind that time. But I am putting no reproach on you, for it is on myself the great blame should be, and from this out I have no more to say to love or friendship or anything but the hard business of the day.

Grania: I will not wait. I will give my thoughts no leave to repent. I will give no time to those two slaves to tell out the way I was scorned!

Finn: The men of the armies will laugh and mock at you, seeing you settle out a new wedding in the shadow of your comrade's wake.

Grania:* There is many a woman lost her lord, and took another, and won great praise in the latter end, and great honour. And why should I be always a widow that went so long a maid? Give me now the crown, till I go out before them, as you offered it often enough. (*She puts it on her head.*) I am going, I am going out now, to show myself before them all, and my hand linked in your own. It is well I brought my golden dress.

Finn: Wait till the darkness of the night, or the dusk of the evening itself.

Grania: No, no. Diarmuid might not see me at that time. He might be gone to some other place. He is surely here now, in this room where he parted from the body—he is lingering there by the hearth. Let him see now what I am doing, and that there is no fear on me, or no wavering of the mind. Open the door now for me!

> (*Finn opens door and they go to the opening, she taking his hand. There is a mocking laugh heard. She falls back and crouches down. Finn tries to raise her.*)

Finn: I thought to leave you and to go from you, and I cannot do it. For we three have been these seven years as if alone in the world; and it was the cruelty and the malice of love made its sport with us, when we thought it was our own way we were taking, driving us here and there, knocking you in between us, like the ball between two goals, and the hurlers being out of sight and beyond the boundaries of the world. And all the three of us have been as if worsted in that play. And now there are but the two of us left, and whether we love or hate one an-other, it is certain I can never feel love or hatred for any other woman from this out, or you your-self for any other man. And so as to yourself and myself, Grania, we must battle it out to the end.

(*Finn raises her up. A louder peal of laughter is heard.*)

Grania: (*Going towards the door.*) It is but the armies that are laughing! I thought I heard Diarmuid's laugh.

Finn: It is his friends in the armies gave out that mocking laugh.

Grania: And is it not a poor thing, strong men of the sort to be mocking at a woman has gone through sharp anguish, and the break-ing of love, on this day? Open the door again for me. I am no way daunted or afraid. Let them laugh their fill and welcome, and laugh

you, Finn, along with them if you have a mind.
And what way would it serve me, their praise
and their affection to be mine? For there is not
since an hour ago any sound would matter at
all, or be more to me than the squeaking of bats
in the rafters, or the screaming of wild geese
overhead!

> (*She opens the door herself. Finn puts his
> arm about her. There is another great
> peal of laughter, but it stops suddenly
> as she goes out.*)

Curtain

KINCORA

PERSONS

Malachi . . . HIGH KING OF IRELAND
Maelmora . KING OF LEINSTER, BROTHER TO
GORMLEITH
Brennain . . . . . BRIAN'S SERVANT
Rury . . . . . MALACHI'S SERVANT
Phelan . . . . MAELMORA'S SERVANT
Brian . . KING OF MUNSTER, AFTERWARDS
HIGH KING
Murrough . . . . . . HIS SON
Gormleith . HIS WIFE, FORMERLY MALACHI'S
WIFE
Sitric . . HER SON BY OLAF OF THE DANES
A Beggar Girl

Act I

Scene: A room in Brian's palace at Kincora. Malachi and Maelmora at a table.

Malachi: Brian may be a great man, Maelmora, and he may have earned a great name. But he had n't a stim of sense, no more than I myself, when it came to the choosing of a wife.

Maelmora: Let you keep in mind now when you speak of Brian's wife, it is of my own sister you are speaking.

Malachi: It is hard to keep that in mind and very hard. It is as if something went crossways in the making of the two of you, the way you turned out peaceable, and she that is a woman to be giddy and full of stir. I give you my word you would have as much ease being in the one house with her, as to be lodging in a nest of wild bees.

Maelmora: You took her on the wrong side always, crossing and criticising her, and tormenting her to attend to the needle and to the business of the house. Brian will make a better hand of his marriage, letting her go her own way, and believing as he does there are not her three equals in the world wide.

Malachi: I gave her a good house and good means and a good name the day I made her the High King's wife. Was not that enough to satisfy any woman within the ring of Ireland? And when she turned her hand to meddling with my own business, and with things she had no call to at all, I said good-morrow to her and made a good provision for her; and the Pope of Rome gave her, or did not give her, leave to go suit herself better in a man.

Maelmora: She is getting a good man, getting Brian.

Malachi: That it may come happy! I had enough of that tongue of hers that has the grey scrape of the Spring. I did not begrudge her to Brian the time she came to him, herself, her coach, and her bridesmaids. It is well if we get through the business that brought us here without her. Brian is a hard man, and very hard, at making his own bargain, without having her at his back.

Maelmora: It would be more answerable to us getting time to see our own advisers at home. What chance have we against him, and he in his own place at Kincora?

Malachi: What chance had we against him since the time he brought his fleet of boats up the Shannon? You know well he threatened myself in my own strong place in Meath. It is little chance you yourself had, the time he went following you into Leinster. It is well for you he joined with your sister, or you would have been swept before this.

Maelmora: Hard as they are, he said he would not move from these terms. But it is likely he might come around to give in a little here or there.

Malachi: Every man has a right to do that, and not to push things too far. It would be a queer rope that would not be slackened at one time or another.

Maelmora: He lays down that I myself must be under him, outside such things as concern my own district, and make no league or bargain on my account with any king in or outside of Ireland. But I have made out a new agreement here. Let him leave me to go my own way until there will be some time of need, and then I will come of my free will, and bring all the choice men of Leinster to his help.

Malachi: He wrote in my own agreement that he must have entire authority in Munster and in the whole of the South. He goes so far as to say he can call for judgments to be given here in his own place. I now am not inclined to give in to that. So long as I am High King, I must have every law and every decree given out in Tara.

Maelmora: He is entirely too hard on Sitric. If he is head of the Danes itself, he is my own sister's son, and I must see that he will get fair play. His people should get better treatment, and not be set labouring in the fields and dragging the same as four-footed beasts.

(*Brennain, Rury, and Phelan come in.*
Brennain pulls forward his master's
chair. Brian comes in and sits down.)

Malachi: I myself and the King of Leinster are ready for you now, Brian.

Brian: Is Sitric here, or is there any sign of him coming?

Maelmora: He cannot be far off. There was news he will be here within the hour.

Brian: But you yourselves have put your names to the agreements we made out. Give me yours here, Maelmora.

Maelmora: I did not put my name to it yet. I made some changes. I was thinking you are too hard on me in this.

Brian: You did not think that way the time my army was visiting you in Leinster. Your memory is gone from you in its track. You came asking and calling to me to quit your province, saying you would give in to anything I might lay down. No, there is no cause for that flush on your face. It was only some little forgetfulness. We could find a cure for it quick enough, if I should come again upon the plains of Kildare.

Maelmora: Give it here, I will put my name to what you wrote. (*Signs.*)

Brian: And what about Sitric? You will remember you went bail for him?

Maelmora: If I did I will hold to it. What have we to do? It is you yourself have the power. It is as well to be under you, and to get your protection for ourselves.

Brian: You see how the High King is not slow or unwilling putting his name to his own agreement. No, he has not written it. Brennain, go seek a better pen for the High King's use. It is the pen that has failed, and not his own word. Malachi is like myself, he always holds to his word.

Malachi: (*Signing.*) Well, Brian, you are a hard man. But you are doing what I suppose I myself might be doing, and I being in your place. I sounded the pipes yesterday, you are sounding them to-day. There, you have an equal share of Ireland with myself.

Brian: That is right now. Yourself and myself between us can sweep the whole country, and turn it all to peace.

Malachi: You are a terrible wicked man, Brian, to go out fighting with for peace.

Brian: It is nothing less than that I have been fighting for, through the most of my lifetime, up to now.

Maelmora: I cannot make out at all why so hardy and so dreaded a man should have his mind set on doing away with war.

Brian: It is because I have had my fill of it. Through all the generations my race was for fighting, my father, and my old father, and all that went before. Lugaidh son of Aengus, Cathal son of Aedh, Corc son of Anluan, Lorcan son of Lochta, Cennedigh son of Lorcan; there was no one of them all was reared to any other trade. What way did I myself pass my early time? Watching and attacking, through long winter nights and long summer days, striving to drive out altogether the enemies of Ireland and of Munster. It is well I have earned the right by this to turn from wicked to kind.

Malachi: If there is any man at all can turn peaceable and keep his name up, it is yourself should be able to do it, for there is no one can say it was through any slackness you are doing it, or any fear, for that is a thing never came into the one house with you.

Brian: In troth it is a scarce thing among us. To go into danger shouting, the feet as if rising

off the ground with the stir put in them by
the pipes, the heart airy in the same way, there is
no common man of our armies but will feel that
much, the time the troops of his enemies are coming at him, with their attacks and with their
cries.

Malachi: That is an easy courage enough. It
is a harder thing to hold to what is won, and to
keep out meddlers, and to force respect for the
law. To work that out, and to sweat it out,
watching and foreseeing through the day, the
heart starting and uneasy in the night time, that
is a heavy load for any man to be carrying through
the weeks and the months and the years.

Brian: There is no one in this country hardy
enough to face it out but the two, or maybe
the three, of us in this room. And as to myself,
it is long ago I might have run from it, but for
respect for the Man that laid the charge on me,
that is God.

Malachi: It is often I thought there was a
good saint spoiled in you, Brian, and you taking
to the straight sword and not to the Bishop's
crook.

Murrough: It might have been better for
yourself, Malachi, if my father had never meddled
with a sword.

Malachi: Hearken to the crowing of the young
cock! We are done with all that now, Murrough.

The sparrows are nesting to-day that were scolding at one another yesterday.

Brian: (*Getting up and looking out.*) It is a pity Sitric is not come to make an entire end of this business.

Maelmora: I tell you I am answerable for my nephew Sitric. He is giving in altogether.

Malachi: He had nothing to do but to give in, the time you took away the help of Leinster from him.

Maelmora: I will go out by the Hill of the Grey Rock to meet him. It is likely he may be coming by Lough Graney. I promised him a good welcome from you, Brian.

Brian: You did well promising that. Go you, Murrough, with Maelmora. I myself will go towards the weir. He might chance to come from the south.

Malachi: I will go along with you, Brian. We can be pricing the colts in the river meadows as we go.

Brian: (*To Brennain.*) Make the table ready, Brennain. When Sitric comes all we have to do is to see his name put to the agreement, and to sit down to dinner.

(*The Kings all go out. The servants come forward.*)

Phelan: This peace is a great celebration now of Brian's wedding with Queen Gormleith. Ma-

lachi the High King owning the whole of the
North. Brian King of the whole of the South!
Maelmora safe in his own place in Leinster.
Meddling with one another no more than the
white and the yolk of an egg! Peace as round
and as sound as the eggshell itself. Peace forever in Ireland and Leinster and in Kincora!

Brennain: Ah, what signifies talking about eggs
and about agreements? The one is as perishable
as the other. Believe me there is some mother
of mischief does be always at roost overhead in
Ireland, to claw and to shatter pacifications or any
well disposed thing at all. Peaces and treaties! I
would make no treaty with the Gall but to
strike their head off!

Phelan: You are always ready, Brennain, to
put ridicule upon anything I will lay down. But
I know well, whatever may have happened at any
other time, this peace will never be broken. Who
is there to frustrate it? It is not the Danes will
do that and they being the way they are, not
daring to let a squeal out of them, no more
than a hunted otter would have gone hiding in
a stream.

Rury: Whoever may break that peace it will
not be my master Malachi. Too wide he is and
too fleshy, and too easy, to be craving more of
the cares and the hardships of the world. It is
quiet he is asking now, to get some comfort and

to train his four-year-olds, and to be sleeping his sound sleep through the night time.

Phelan: Whoever might break the peace it will not be my own master Maelmora. Now that the Danes are beat, he has no mind to be beat along with them, and in my opinion he is right.

Brennain: There is no one but must say that Brian has done his best for peace, and he going so far as to bring home a wife, as a notice and as a sign that the country should be tranquillised. It is not out of Kincora that any provocation will be rising up. Sure our teeth are clogged yet with the leavings of the wedding feast.

Rury: There is no chance I suppose, my hero, that the newly married Queen might bring the pot to the boil?

Brennain: Ah, not at all! What call would she have to be meddling in things of the sort? A very pleasant plain lady, kind and nice and lucky; it 's as easy talk to her as a child.

Phelan: I was wondering not to see her to-day and the kings having that big work in hand. That is not the way she used to be in her early time in Leinster.

Brennain: Spearing eels she went, up in the shallows of the river. A good housekeeper she is. She is not one would take her ease and leave the Friday without provision. And there are many not having as much as her, would n't walk the road with pride.

Rury: You are a very clever man surely Brennain and a good judge of the Queens of the world and their ways.

Brennain: Sure we had a Queen in it previously. Murrough's mother that was a girl of the Hynes out of Connacht. A very nice biddable woman, rocking the cradle with Murrough, and thanking God for her own good luck through the Sundays and holidays of the year. And what Brian got at the first offer, it is not likely it will fail him secondly, and he being high up in the world, and getting sense and experience through up to near three-score years.

Phelan: Stop your mouth now. Here she is herself coming up the path from the river side. Stepping on the tops of the grass she is, as if she never felt the weight of her crosses; and she a widow-woman before Malachi joined with her itself.

(Gormleith comes to threshold and stands looking in. All the servants fall back and bow obsequiously.)

Brennain: A welcome before you, Queen, and that you may keep your luck ever and always; and what you have not to-day, that you may have ten times more this day twenty years!

Gormleith: *(Giving him her eel-spear and net.)*

6

Who are these that are come to the house? Is that not Phelan of the King of Leinster's people? You are Rury, King Malachi's serving man. But the High King is not here yet?

Rury: The High King is here these three hours, Queen; he took notice of you in the boat, and you going up the river.

Gormleith: It is likely he is taking some rest, according to his custom.

Rury: He is not, Queen, but he is after doing the business he had taken in hand.

Gormleith: (*Coming to Maelmora's chair, putting her hand on the back of it.*) What put that hurry on him? He used not to be so eager, but slack.

Rury: Troth he made no delay this time, but sent word to Brian it was best to make a start and to finish the work out of face. Himself and Maelmora sat down after that, and never quitted arguing and sounding out the writings they had put down, till such time as they had their agreement made out with Brian.

Gormleith: (*To Phelan.*) Did my brother agree to this new bargain?

Phelan: He did agree where he had to agree to it, and Malachi that had him led to make a stand against Brian, giving in and agreeing on his own side.

Gormleith: He had a right to have come to

me for advice.   Maelmora is as simple and as innocent as a child.

Phelan: It is a pity indeed he to have joined in with Malachi at all.

Gormleith: What now has Malachi himself got out of this?   Did the High Kingship slip from him yet?

Rury: Malachi is High King now and always, and with the help of God he will be King in Tara to the end.

Gormleith: What part have the Danes now in the new agreement?   Is Sitric given any share in the country?

Phelan: Sitric is to be forced to quit the country before the quarter, and his troop of Danes along with him, or to be under the jurisdiction of Malachi and of Brian.

Gormleith: I was never told that.   Did Sitric agree to be banished, or to take orders from Malachi?

Phelan: It is what I heard them saying, he will give in to stop here under orders.   Maelmora, that went security, said he would write his name to that treaty of pacification, between this and the fall of night.

Gormleith: They did not forewarn me he was coming.   I thought the business would not be pressed on in this way.

Phelan: It is for himself they are waiting at

this time. They are gone out to hurry him, and they are right doing that. He to make any more delay, it will not be answerable to the dinner.

Gormleith: They will be wanting their dinner after such great work. I am greatly in your way, Brennain. You had best make ready the tables.

Brennain: All is ready and waiting, Queen. We have but to set the chairs, and to bring in the dishes that are dressed.

Gormleith: I do not see you stirring yourself, Rury. Is there no help you can give?

Rury: I can be putting the chair ready for the High King. (*Pulls a chair forward.*)

Gormleith: Do not put that chair for him, that is King Brian's chair.

Rury: It is the custom to give the best chair to the High King of Ireland.

Gormleith: It was the custom. But remember the High King is not above King Brian now. He is but his equal. They are the Kings of the North and the South.

Rury: I would never give in to put Malachi below any other man at all.

Phelan: Where can I put the King of Leinster's chair?

Brennain: Put it there—by Malachi's left hand. That is it. A little farther down.

Gormleith: You are putting it too close, Phelan. King Malachi is so high over all, there must be the length of a sword left between him and any other King of a Province.

Phelan: My master is good enough to sit close up to any one of the kings of the world.

Gormleith: (*To Rury.*) You should put these forgetful men in mind that your master is master over them.

Rury: So he is, so he is! It is Tara is the capital of Ireland.

Brennain: It is not, but Kincora that is the capital.

Phelan: (*At window.*) There is Sitric coming; himself and the King of Leinster are on the brow of the hill.

Brennain: It is best for us to be putting the meat on the table so. (*Goes to the door, and brings back dishes one by one from outside.*) Sitric will sign his name with the less delay the time he will see the fat of the mutton hardening.

Gormleith: (*Who has gone to the window, turning from it.*) They are a long way off. I will go meet them. You have time enough. I will leave you an advice. Be sure that the best dish is set before the greatest of the Kings. (*Goes out.*)

Brennain: Here is the best dish, the salted round of the beef. I will set it here before King Brian.

Rury: It is before Malachi it has a right to

be put. The best dish should be put before the High King.

Brennain: You heard what Queen Gormleith is after saying, that Brian is every bit as good now as Malachi.

Rury: He is not as good as the King of Tara; and he never will be as good. Put the beef here.

Brennain: Here is a dish is as good, a roasted quarter of a boar.

Rury: We have plenty of pigs in the North. A pig is no great dish for a King. The beef is the more honourable dish.

Brennain: If it is, it is to the more honourable man it is going.

Rury: How do you make that out? The High King is the most honourable man.

Brennain: The High King is it? Where would he be this day but for Brian?

Rury: What is that you are saying?

Brennain: I tell you if it was not for Brian taking the Danes in hand the way he did, it is hares of the wilderness Malachi might be looking for milk from to-morrow morning, instead of from cows!

Rury: Brian is it? Where was Brian the day Malachi took the golden collar from the big Dane? Answer me that!

Brennain: That Malachi may be choked with that same collar before the size of my

nail of this beef will go down his gullet until
he has asked it first of Brian!

Rury: Asked it of Brian!

Brennain: Asked it and begged it, the same
as a queen's lapdog begs at the table.

Phelan: And what share of the meat is the
King of Leinster to get? It is another round
of the beef should be put before him!

Brennain: The next time the King of Leinster
comes here he will find his fill of beef before him—
his own cattle that will be coming from now to
then, as tribute from the traitors of Leinster!

Phelan: Holy Saint Brigit! Listen to what
they are saying of your own province!

Rury: Brennain is right that time. Tripe and
cow-heels and pigs' crubeens are good enough for
that troop, and too good!

Phelan: Oh, let me out of this! Tripe and
crubeens, and all that plenty in the house. I will
call upon all the poets of Leinster to put the curse
of scarcity on Kincora!

Brennain: My grief I have not the time to
sharpen this knife. No matter. It is on your
own bones I will sharpen it. (*All seize knives
and threaten each other. Maelmora, Murrough,
Sitric, and Gormleith come in.*)

Murrough: Have the dogs been let loose from
the kennels? Brennain, what is the meaning of
these noises?

Brennain: It is those ones that made an attack on me. For quiet I myself am, and for getting ready the table.

Phelan: Taking the best of the beef he was, and leaving my master to the culls.

Brennain: It was Rury that was asking the best of the chairs for Malachi.

Rury: Let you keep your chair so! Malachi will be master in whatever chair he may sit.

Murrough: Malachi master here! That is a new thing for us to know.

Phelan: Some say he is uppermost, and some say Brian, but the King of Leinster is put in the lowest place of all.

Maelmora: (*To Murrough.*) Am I thought to be so greatly below Brian, on the head of agreeing to a settlement with him?

Murrough: You agreed to pay rent for your province. It is not the one is uppermost that sends in a rent.

Maelmora: If Brian had spoken in that way I would not have given in to send it. I have a mind to keep it back even now.

Murrough: If we send our men looking for it, there will be maybe more profit with us than with yourself.

Maelmora: I am well able to hold my province against the men of Kincora. Let them fish and shiver like cranes in moonlight, before they

will see so much as one staggering bullock
coming from Leinster.

Sitric: (*To Maelmora.*) You made out it
was for peacemaking you brought me here. It
seems to me more like the making of a battle.

Gormleith: If that is so, it might happen as
lucky. You are in your early days, it might
chance you to make a better fight for yourself.

Sitric: It is a great pity I came to Kincora
without bringing a good back of my own men.

Murrough: If you had come bringing your
fleet of Danes, it is likely you might have got a
welcome would have kept you here until the
brink of Judgment!

Sitric: It would have been right to have smoked
out this den in the winter nights that are past.

Murrough: That smoke would have brought
us out to do what was done on you at Sulcoit.

Gormleith: (*To Maelmora.*) It was your advice that brought Sitric here. Are you satisfied he
is getting good treatment and a friend's welcome?

Maelmora: Keep your tongue quiet, Murrough.
It is hardly Sitric will bear from you, what he
might bear from Brian.

Sitric: I will take no scolding salute from
Brian or from any other man, whatever you
yourself may be in the habit of taking.

Maelmora: I have no such habit. I will not
let any man say that.

Sitric: You have taken his orders, you are dragging me into his service the same as yourself.

Maelmora: If I joined in his league it might happen to me to break away from it yet. It might be less troublesome after, even if it should bring me to my death.

Murrough: There is many a man met with a woeful death through setting himself up against King Brian.

Brennain: That is good talk, Murrough! It is Brian has the sway in every place! It is Murrough, my darling, and Brian, are the two hawks of battle of the Gael!

Phelan: It is myself and Maelmora will turn you to jackdaws! It is ourselves will change your note for you!

Rury: Malachi and the Hill of Tara!

Brennain: Kincora and the River Shannon!

Phelan: No rent to Brian! We 'll hold the cattle!

Rury: Hi for Tara!

Brennain: Out with the Meath graziers!

Phelan: Down with Kincora!

Brennain: No, but down with Leinster! (*Murrough, Sitric, and Maelmora are striking at one another with their swords.*)

Rury: The Kings! (*Murrough, Maelmora, and Sitric draw back as Brian and Malachi come in. The servants fall back.*)

Brian: (*Sternly.*) Murrough, what ails you? Are these mannerly ways?

Murrough: (*Suddenly taking hand from sword.*) It is you they were faulting, and Kincora. They gregged me with their threats and their jibes. They said they were as great as you. They said—I forget now what they said.

Brian: Shut your ears, Murrough, to stiff words said under your own roof. It is best not to hear what you have no leave to answer. (*To Sitric and Malachi.*) I ask your pardon—I am sorry such a thing has happened.

> (*He goes aside with them. Malachi and Gormleith meet.*)

Malachi: (*To Gormleith.*) I got no chance before this to salute the Queen of Munster.

Gormleith: She is very thankful to King Malachi for the Godspeed that was said to her in Tara.

Malachi: It would seem that you have found in Kincora the stir it failed you to find in my own house.

Gormleith: It is likely I would have found stir if I had stopped with you for another while, and yourself and myself facing one another on the hearthside, through the dark evenings of the year.

Malachi: It would be no wonder, in my opinion, if the Queen herself had put the kindling to this crackling wisp?

Gormleith: I would not put a lie on the High King, whatever opinion he might be giving out.

Malachi: Mind now, Queen, what I am going to say. I am not joking or funning. You are come into a good man's house. Give heed to your flighty headstrong ways, or it may happen you some day to put kindling to no less a thing than the roof that gave shelter to you.

Brian: (*Coming over to them.*) I am sorry, Queen, you have seen such disorder in this place, and you being in it so short a while. You will bring order into it now. I had to straighten out my own home, or it would fail me to shape the whole country to the one pattern. A house without a good woman over it is no better than a busy hillside, where men are shouting, and hounds are snapping at their prey, and mannerly ways are out of mind.

Gormleith: Indeed I have no complaint to make of all that I have found before me.

Brian: It is seldom a woman's voice was heard here through the years past, unless it might be in the keening, when the dead of our race are brought home.

Gormleith: It is no sleepy place I am come to, or a place where slackness would be in fashion. I am satisfied and well satisfied with the roof that has given me shelter.

Malachi: Let us not be wasting time now,

and the day going. Sitric is here with us. Let him put his name to the agreement, and the dinner will turn the whole company to better humour. Good meat and good drink are maybe the best peacemakers.

Brian: There is the agreement, Sitric. Maelmora, your uncle, put down the terms you had settled between you. You have but to put your name. The securities will be written with it to-morrow. (*Sitric is silent.*) Will you cast an eye on it? Or are you satisfied with whatever Maelmora has written?

Malachi: We put down in the writing that you and your army would agree to quit Ireland or to live in quiet, without arms, in the service of myself and of Brian.

Sitric: I will not write my name to it.

Brian: You came here promising to do it.

Malachi: It was of your own free will you sent in your submission. Why would you draw back from it now?

Sitric: Words have been said to me that I am not used to put up with.

Brian: This is Murrough's foolishness. I have asked your pardon for it, and he will ask your pardon.

Sitric: I will not agree to obey or give in to any one of you at all.

Malachi: What is that you are saying?

Sitric: I will not give in to yourself or to Brian. I will not give in to be a stranger and an exile. I will not bid my people to give up their arms. I will bid them to go on fighting to the last.

Brian: You know well you could not stand against us alone, through the length of a winter day.

Maelmora: He will not be alone. I give up my share in this league. I would sooner be with the Danes, than under Brian of the Tributes.

Malachi: How quick you youngsters are at taking offence! A couple of foolish words said, and all our trouble gone to loss. When you are as long on the road as we are you will take things easy. In my opinion Brian was too soft with the two of you up to this. It would have been better to have banished you, and gained some comfort for the both of us. (*To Brian.*) Maybe we can make them some offer. Let them have their own way with Leinster so long as they will not meddle with ourselves. A new war would be a weighty business. You were saying awhile ago the country was in great need of peace.

Brian: Entire peace is what is badly wanting, but a half peace is no better worth the winning than the half of the living child was brought to the Judgment of Solomon.

Malachi: In my opinion you will not see

entire peace or the end of quarrels in Ireland,
till such time as the grass stops growing or talk
comes to the thrush.

Brian: I tell you I will make no settlement
that will leave any one of the five Provinces a
breeding ground for the enemies and the ill-
wishers of Ireland. When Charlemagne of the
French took his work in hand he left no such a
nest of mischief; or Harold in Norway, or Alfred
of the burned cakes, that is in the histories.
This tossed tormented country has to be put
in order, and to be kept in order, and travel
whatever road God laid out for it, without arguing and backbiting and the quarrelling of cranky
bigoted men. Sitric must put his name to this
or make himself ready for a battle and a check.

Sitric: (*Takes parchment, looks at it a moment,
then cuts it through with his sword and throws it down
violently.*) There is an end of your agreement!

Brian: (*Taking out sword.*) This edge is sharp
yet. God knows I am telling no lie saying I
would sooner see it rusted than raddled.

Malachi: War is a troublesome business.
There is maybe no one of us will be the
better of it in the end.

Brian: (*Unbuckling sheath.*) But as to this
cover it may rust and rot, for I will make no
use of it from this out so long as there is so much
as a whisper of rebellion or of treachery in any

province or barony or parish, east or west, north or south! (*Throws it down.*)

Sitric: Let my own stay with it till I come to bring it away! (*Throws down sheath.*)

Maelmora: And there is mine along with it! (*He and Sitric turn to go.*)

Gormleith: (*To Malachi.*) That is the way we strike the board till we see the cards coming to us! The trump will be in our hands yet! Are you loth, Malachi, to trust your luck to the cards? Do not be daunted, Brian is on your side this time! But believe me, the world will wonder yet, at the luck you let go from you to Brian!

Curtain

Act II

Scene: Same room at Kincora. Heap of spoils on floor. Brennain has just come in holding Phelan, who is bound. Music outside and shouting. Rury is looking at spoils on floor.

Brennain: Those are terrible great shouts the people are letting out of them to welcome King Brian, that has beat the whole fleet of traitors at Glenmama, and has them ground as fine as meal!

Rury: And to welcome King Malachi that beat them along with him, and that will be here within the hour.

Brennain: And maybe to welcome myself! What now do you say to me taking this prisoner in the battle! Drove him before me I did the whole of the way from Glenmama. Believe me it 's the Leinster men can run well!

Rury: Is it my brave Phelan is in it, that went out such a hero to the war?

Brennain: (*Pushing Phelan before him.*) Come on here! Is it that you said we were jackdaws? Give me a wisp of lighted straw, till I'll make him shout for King Brian!

Rury: That's the chat! That's the chat! Put terror on him now, till he'll let out a shout for the High King!

Brennain: That's the way we drag traitors back, that went boasting and barging out of Kincora.

Phelan: If I did boast, you need not be putting the blame on myself. The dog to get a bone, the dog's tail must wag. I do but wag as my master pleases.

Brennain: (*Looking at heap of spoils.*) It is ourselves are nourished with the bone presently! Satin stuffs, gold rings, jewels would buy out the entire world! Coming in since morning they are! You would not meet a car or a Christian on the road but is charged with them! Robbed by the Danes they were from every strong place in Ireland and from the hidden houses of the Sidhe!

Rury: I am best pleased my own mind to be dwelling on the prisoners. Sitric to be taken with his army of Danes. The King of Leinster to be brought here (*turns to Phelan*) spancelled in a gad, the same as his own serving man.

Brennain: It was Murrough took him, my darling boy! Concealed he was in a yew tree.

It was Murrough dragged him out of it, the same as a wren's nest.

Phelan: It is very unmannerly you are, to be casting up that yew tree against the King of Leinster. Sure he not to go hide in it, he might not be at this time in the living world.

Rury: What now will Queen Gormleith have to say, her son and her brother the same as judged and executed, and the whole of their means made our prey.

Phelan: That is a thing will not happen. I tell you, that is a lady is well able to bring a man from the foot of the gallows. She is not one would leave it to God to rule the world, the time she herself has a hand to put to the work.

Brennain: Brian that was turning to be kind will not show kindness this time. He took it very bad, Maelmora and Sitric to stand up to him the way they did, and he after binding them by an act of peace. It is not consanguinity will save Queen Gormleith's brother, or get off her lad of a son.

Phelan: She will gain safety for him, and for the two of them, through some enticement or some strategy of her own. It is easy seen, Brennain, that you were never joined with a wife.

Brennain: If I was itself, there is no woman or no score of women, cranky or civil, coaxer or

cross, would ever put me from my own opinion,
I once to have laid it down.

Phelan: It is likely Brian will give in to the
asking of the woman he will have beside him
through the length of the four quarters of the
year. Whinging and whining she will come to
him; making threats she will go perish on their
grave. I tell you there are women in it, would
coax the entire world.

Rury: And what way would it profit her, striving to influence Brian? Sure there is no one has
power to judge and to chastise these prisoners at
all, but only the High King, that is Malachi.

Brennain: It is a bad chastisement he will be
apt to be giving them. Brian would be severe
on no person if there was anything at all to be
said for him. But as to a wind from the North,
it will never be civil or kind.

Rury: It will no way serve her to come pur-
ring around Malachi. She knows that well herself. It is more likely a taste she will give him of
the sharpness of her claws.

Phelan: The Lord be with Malachi she to set
herself against him, in earnest! She would have
him out of the High Kingship between this and
the roosting of the hens.

Rury: It is not likely Brian would be asking
to earn the name of a grabber, snapping up the
High Kingship for himself.

Brennain: If he did grab it, he would turn it to better profit than what Malachi is doing. What signifies a High King that is satisfied with such things as may come into his hand, without any sort of big thoughts and of lofty plans? Brian now would stand at his own hall door and cast an eye over the whole of the domains of the world and Tir-nan-oge along with them. To get this country pacified, the way he could work out all that he had in his mind, that is what set him cracked and craving after peace. I never knew him to be disconcerted but the day that last treaty was tore. "Give me twenty year, or ten year itself, of quiet," says he to the Queen, "and the world will bow down to the name of Ireland." "Give us the High Kingship," says I to myself with myself, "and we will find something more to do with it, than to go racing garrans in Meath."

Rury: No fear of you getting it. It was sealed and witnessed in the bond, Malachi to preserve it for his lifetime.

Brennain: Brian to get it, he would make Ireland the leader of the universe! The men of arts from every part coming to learn their own trade; coming by shoals they would be, like mackerel on the spring tide! Every smith of a forge shaping golden bracelets! Every scholar in a school speaking the seven languages! Every village of cabins a city with towers and with walls! Towers am I saying, no but rounded steeples would penetrate the thunder in the clouds.

Rury: Well you are great old warriors for giving out boasting talk in Kincora.

Brennain: It is Brian will put his orders on the ocean, on the narrow seas and the wide! His ships will go searching out every harbour! Every strange sail will moult and wither, getting a sight of his lime-white sail. He will put his rent on the kings of the world, they will pay him a heavy rent!

Rury: Pride grew in you, as rank as cabbage of the young moon, since you chancing on a straggler of your own!

Brennain: Rents they will send, and tributes they will send! Sea-horses having blue eyes, barrels broke and bursting with the weight of rendered gold! Elephants' teeth, hairy men, and peacocks, the same as to Solomon of the Jews.

Phelan: It was a woman's wit baffled King Solomon at the end, the time he thought to drive her from his house. What is Queen Gormleith apt to be at all that time? Do you think will she be satisfied to be sitting quiet, and her thoughts near as flighty as your own?

Brennain: She will be satisfied and tethered and clogged, with the sight of the grandeur all around! There is no woman at all but would be subjugated, and all the nations to be blowing the horn before her man.

Rury: (*Looks out of window. A shout outside.*)
There is King Brian himself at the door, and
the people going cracked after him. Malachi
should be on the road yet. I see no sign of
him coming. It is best for me to go ask news
of him, and be getting a shout for him by the
time he will come in view. (*Goes out.*)

(*Brennain pushes Phelan off through door.
Brian comes in, goes slowly to his chair.*)

Brennain: The Branch to King Brian! All
the people are gone wild for you! The poets are
starting a poem about the great victory of
Glenmama! A song with as many verses as my
fingers and toes, and a great deed in every verse.

Brian: That it may be a good one, for if
I get my own way I will give them no cause to
make songs from this out, on the head of
battles or of slaughter.

Brennain: Good is it? The words are coming as fast as the running of the Danes before
us! Making for the sea they were the same as
gulls; they are putting the screaming of gulls in
the poem.

Brian: Let them twang it a long way off! I
have had enough of noises. (*Sits down and takes
off sword.*)

Brennain: What will we do with the treasures
we brought away? The whole place is choked
up with them.

Brian: Make three shares of them. A share for the High King, and a share for the learned men, and a share for Kincora.

Brennain: I will, I will keep the best share for ourselves.

Brian: The best must go to the High King.

Brennain: It is you yourself have a right to be High King, Brian, after this great victory. I tell you all Ireland is thirsting for it.

Brian: I know, I know, they were sounding it out on the roads. They are calling out against two kings being in the one saddle. But they may deafen themselves with shouting before they will make me break my peace with Malachi.

Brennain: They 'd sooner you. It is not Malachi will master the five provinces, tearing and spitting at one another the way they are. Five wild cats struggling in a bag, and four times five claws on every one of them.

Beggar: (*At door.*) In the name of Brigit is beside me with her cloak,

In the name of Michael is before me with his power,

MacDuagh, MacDara, and Columcille of my love,

I put this house under the power of the Man having the candle!

Brian: Who is that?

Brennain: Some travelling woman carrying

the bag—the heavy sweat running down beside her—she should have been running on her road. (*Beggar comes in.*) What is it brings you here? What call have you coming here, you that are used to ditches and to haggards, to be standing on the royal threshold of the King?

Brian: It is sometimes those that go sleeping on the straw of a haggard have their own view of the angels of heaven. You would seem not to have got any long sleep in any place. Where was it you spent the night-time?

Beggar: Last night at the feet of the poor,
To-morrow at the feet of the Son of God.

I ran fast, and very fast, to come as far as yourself, Brian.

Brian: What is it makes you so uneasy?

Beggar: Looking I am for the hidden key. Go search it out yourself, King Brian, in this day of your great victory.

For all you have won of silver and of store,
And the people raising you in their arms,
Let you be remembering bye and bye,
Let you do your ploughing for the harvest in
    heaven!

Brian: God knows I have ears for that call if the hurry of the times did not hold me.

Beggar: Come searching for the key of heaven. It is in some hidden vessel.

Come out before your candle will be spent,

At the asking of the Man beyond, the King of
Sunday.

Make yourself ready for the day of the Mountain,

Before your lease will be out and your summons
written!

Brian: It is the wanderers of the world should
be happy, being freed as they are to run that
road. I myself am a labouring man under orders,
having the weight of this (*holding up sword*)
in my hands through the days and the hours and
the months and the years.

Beggar: Any labouring man at all would be
free to throw down the scythe at the end of
the day, and the bell ringing.

Brian: In my contract, the Saturday night is
all one with the Monday morning. It is the King
of the Angels gave this to me. It is with it I am
striving to cut the name of Ireland in clean letters among the nations. It is with this I have
to do my work, until such time as the poor
class, the people that are very sorry, will get
some ease and some comfort and some wealth.

Beggar: You are out of it! You are out of
it! Bruise the ground and that will be done
for you. Put that weighty thing out of your
hand. Take in place of it nine drops of the
water of wisdom—bring down Adam's paradise
till we have it about us on every side; teach

all the people to be telling the hours, till they have their eyes clear to see the angels walking Ireland in plenty!

Brian: I will surely turn to no other work, the time I will have freed the whole of the country from all keening and mischief and treachery. It is to bring that time I have stooped my back till now from the rising of the sun.

Beggar: That that time may come soon and come happy!

Brian: Look now at that ring. It is worth great riches. Take it and give me your prayers. Bring me word that a lone woman can walk Ireland carrying a ring like that, and no one troubling her, and I will take it as a sign I am given leave to sit down at the table of the angels.

Beggar: I will do that, I will do that for you. I will run and run till I will loosen your mind from its cares. My grief that I am not a salmon to go leaping through the streams of Ireland to bring news there is no blemish on its peace, or a crane to go flying in the same way. My grief that I have but these two bare feet. (*Takes ring and turns to go.*)

Brigit of victories, put your cloak around me,
Come, Michael Oge, and take me by the hand,
O bush of shelter, O well reared archangel,
Come travel beside me over ridges, over bogs!

Gormleith: (*Coming in.*) Brennain, take away
this poor woman from the place she has no right
to be, let her sit with the other beggars at the
gate or give her a charity and let her go. Leave
me here with the King. (*Brennain and beggar
go out.*)

Brian: Ah, my Queen, I had sent for you.
Have you no welcome before me?

Gormleith: A welcome and a great welcome
to you, Brian.

Brian: It is in your words—but your face
gives no good welcome. You are not looking
flowery, but pale.

Gormleith: There has heavy news reached to
me, that has put me to and fro.

Brian: No wonder in that, my poor Gormleith.
I your own comrade on the one side, and your
own blood and kindred on the other side, there
must trouble fall upon you, whatever side is
uppermost.

Gormleith: The trouble is gone from me.
You are back here with me, and you are not
looking vexed but kind.

Brian: My dear, you are nearer to me than
my heart.

Gormleith: I knew there would be no fear,
you being in the one house with me again.

Brian: There will be nothing to call us from
one another from this out. We have a great

work to do for this country together. Our best
time is coming, and our shining time.

Gormleith: And you will not refuse me my
first request?

Brian: You had no request to make up to
this, because I gave all before your asking.
Tell me what is it you are wanting from me
now?

Gormleith: You will put no hard punishment
on Maelmora and on Sitric? You will not banish
them out of Ireland? You will forgive them?
You will let them go free?

Brian: As for myself, the time of hardness is
behind me. But you are forgetting it is not by
me they must be judged.

Gormleith: Ah, but whisper now, you will
do it this time, you will make some way to bring
it about? You would not see me fretting, fretting, after my son that is my darling—and
my brother?

Brian: It is the High King has to be judge.

Gormleith: Malachi? Then they are the same
as lost! What chance will they have facing him?
He will be bitter against them on my account.

Brian: You are not right saying that. It is
given in to Malachi that he is a fair man and an
honest man.

Gormleith: It is not my son will get fair play
from him. Judge him yourself, Brian, and give

him the punishment you think right, and whatever it is I will make no complaint.

Brian: I would be glad and very glad to comfort you, but that is a thing cannot be done.

Gormleith: You are a great man and a great king. You can do everything. Give in to this now, and it is not to-day or to-morrow I will serve you, but every day.

Brian: What I can give I have given, without any interest or any bargain.

Gormleith: Why would you give in to Malachi? Through this while past he is lessening, you are strengthening, there is no one but will say you are the strongest.

Brian: The law is stronger again. It is the law that the High King must judge kings and makings of kings.

Gormleith: That is a crooked law. Break away from it, Brian.

Brian: Give heed to me now, I agreed to the laws and swore to them, and I will not be the one to turn and to renage. You would have no good opinion of me yourself, Gormleith, I doing that.

Gormleith: Then it is certain they will be sent to their death.

Brian: They took the chance of that, and they going into the war. There are many have lost life and all through their work.

Gormleith: He will put me down, putting them down. That will not satisfy him. He will accuse me along with them, he will say I stirred them up. It is best for me to take my place beside them. Let the three of us be judged together.

Brian: That will not happen. The High King himself would not dare to meddle with my wife.

Gormleith: It will be best. It is not to banishment they will be sent. I will go meet my own death with them, with Sitric and with Maelmora. I will not go on living after them. My heart will break in me, and I will die! It is soon we all will be in the ground together.

Brian: I thought the woman I married had more courage in her.

Gormleith: Ah, it is hard to keep courage when trouble comes scalding the heart.

Brian: If they had been killed in any of their battles, you would have keened them, and put a high stone over them, and raised your head again and not given in to grief.

Gormleith: That would have been a good death. But what are they going to now but a poor shameful lonely death? Oh, Maelmora! Oh, Sitric! Oh, dear black head! Oh, my child that I have never wronged! But God be with all the mothers of the world!

Brian: You were brought up in a king's house, you knew the rules of every quarrel and of every game. And you were married into kings' houses, and you should know, whatever hand the cards come into, the game must be played out fair. And those laws and these rules will not be broken, even if they should break a queen's heart, or it might be a king's in its track.

Murrough: (*Coming in.*) Here now is the High King.

Brian: Bring in the prisoners before him. (*Murrough goes out. Gormleith goes back into corner where she is not seen.*)

Malachi: (*Comes in and sits down at table.*) I was delayed on the way. Your Munster roads are good inn-keepers, they would not let the wheels of my chariot go from them.

> (*Murrough comes in with Sitric and Mael-mora bound, followed by Brennain, Rury, and Phelan.*)

Brian: The prisoners are here before you.

Malachi: There is no cause for delay. Their judgment will be a quick one.

Brian: Let it be a merciful one as well as just.

Malachi: It is sometimes what is the hardest to one or to two, is the punishment kindest at the last to the scores and the hundreds.

Brian: Have they any excuse to make for themselves?

Murrough: They have made none to me.

Malachi: There is no excuse for them to make.

Brian: What have you to say in your own defence ?

Murrough: You hear, Maelmora and Sitric, what my father is asking.

Maelmora: I will say no word. I went out fighting, and the fight turned against me.

Sitric: Where is the use of talking? Nothing I could say would turn your mind from whatever you may have planned.

Brian: What do you say, High King?

Malachi: There is nothing to be said, but the story we all know before. These men were bound to peace, they had promised peace. I had need of quiet, Brian was calling for quiet, the whole country was in need of it. The whole of Ireland was a raddled fleece, a flock torn by wild dogs. We that were as if herding, were tired out with keeping them off. We made out an agreement together. I agreed to give up a great deal to Brian for the sake of a settlement, and I held to my word, and they broke their word. There is no one can put trust in them from this out. That is the whole story. Is there a lie in what I have said, Brian?

Brian: There is no lie in it. All you have said is true.

Malachi: You know well what way the law

8

would condemn them; and these have no more
right to law than a dog or a fox from the woods.

Brian: That would mean death.

Malachi: The wild dog that is hanged will
worry no sheep.   The fox that is dead will de-
vour no lambs.

Murrough: They can make no complaint.
They did not spare their own prisoners, or their
rebels.

Gormleith: (*Coming forward.*) Malachi!

Malachi: (*Sternly and rising.*) This is not a
right place for you, or a fitting place.

Gormleith: Malachi, the time you and I myself
parted one from another, there was many a thing
to forgive between us.   Whatever you may have
working in your mind against myself, I beg and
pray you not to let it work against these.

Malachi: God knows, that is above us, there
is nothing in my heart against them, but the
thing all this country that they have wronged
must have against them, the attack made by
them upon the peace of Ireland, and the great
slaughter done by their means at Glenmama.

Gormleith: I will ask no other thing of you
for ever, Malachi, but to stretch out now and to
forgive them.

Malachi: I would wish any other in the whole
world to have made that request, till I would
show it is no grudge or no malice is making

me refuse it, but the great necessity of this country.

Gormleith: Put it from your mind there is any woman before you, but only King Brian's wife. It is a good man's wife is making this asking.

Malachi: It is his own good name I am serving. I am not willing for the people to say, and the generations that are rising, that King Brian came meddling with the laws that are for their protection and their safety. It is not Brian would wish it to be said among the people, it was a woman came around us and misled us.

Gormleith: Ah, if it is to the people you are calling to bear witness, I can tell you what is it the people are saying. They say it is you yourself have the sway, and that it is under your sway all they own has been turned to wrack and to ruin. Yes, Brian, I know what I am saying (*Brian has tried to interrupt her*). In his early days there was no one to beat him, he was wary, he was hardy, he was great. But look now the way things are in his province, and in every place that is under him! No one travelling your highways, but it is in the byroads men must creep, your wheat fields all headland, the children treading on the hungry grass. They are cursing you for that. Oh, I have heard them. They say they would as soon be under the wicked Danes as under Malachi that is turned careless and

turned weak. That is why you will not let off
these enemies that are beaten! You are afraid to
show kindness, you are in dread of those poor
hungry people, you are in dread they would
say, "Take his place away from him, we were
right; Malachi has turned to be weak."

Malachi: You have said one true word,
Gormleith, saying that I am in dread. I am that.
I am afraid to show kindness. And I do not
say but that these two left alone would be apt
to give in, and to carry out their bargain straight
and fair. But they would not do it, and they
would not be let do it. It was I myself brought
you back from the Danes, thinking to turn you
to be loyal as a queen should. And it failed
me to do it, and it will fail Brian, and it has
failed him!

Brian: Take heed what you are saying! You
are coming near to danger saying that.

Malachi: Danger, yes there is danger wherever this woman comes, and I have one question to put to her. The cause of this last war
to be searched out, who is it would be found at
the root of it?

Gormleith: I told you, Brian, he would draw
down this on me, I forewarned you. It is best
for me to take my place between my two. I
will take my chance along with them. (*She
goes between Maelmora and Sitric.*) If the fault

was mine, let me pay the penalty. An unkind word to be thrown at a woman, it is little till it brings down her name altogether. The tree to begin to fade, what is there would bring it around? Malachi, I am willing to take you as my judge. You have accused me, give out the decree against me. Judge me here now on this floor.

Malachi: I have no mind to judge any one at all, in this place. I made a great mistake giving in to come into it at all.

Brian: It was laid down between us, this work was to be done in Kincora.

Malachi: I had no business coming here to be checked and dogged on every side. Tara is the place for judgments, and not the house of a king of a province.

Brian: This is a house that had the name of an honest house, and of a house for fair play to the high-up and to the poor.

Malachi: There is too much meddling in it, meddling that will lead to confusion and the breaking of laws. I lay it on you, Brian, to keep order in the first place in your own home. As to these kinsmen of yours, I will bring them as I had a right to have done at the first, to Tara and before the Council of Tara.

Gormleith: You have very big pride in Tara, Malachi. But all Ireland knows, and you know,

this man could put you out of it to-day if he
would but lift his hand up and give the sign.
It is only his kindness and his good will have left
you up to this the name of being High King.

Malachi: Is that your own opinion, Brian, or
is it but the giddy talk of a woman that is
vexed? If you think yourself equal to me, say it
out, and the two of us will settle the case
together.

Brian: I do say it. I say the time is come
when there can be but one master in Ireland.

Malachi: I agree to that. But whoever has
Tara is master.

Brian: Wherever the greatest strength is, the
Hill of Tara is. My strength has dragged Tara
westward.

Malachi: I will not give in to that. It is
only in Tara I will give from this out any decree
or any judgment.

Brian: Then I will give out my own judgment.
I draw down on Maelmora, King of Leinster,
that he has broken from the league made with
me and the High King of Ireland, and turned
his hand against us. I draw down on Sitric, the
Dane, the great oppression he and his people
have done upon Ireland.

Murrough: I will tell our men outside they
have your orders to come in and to bring them
to their death.

Brian: They have earned death and well earned it. They have nothing to urge against it. But stop! Let no one meddle with them! I will leave them their liberty and their life.

Malachi: If Brian had not said that, I would say a fool had said it.

Brian: I am strong enough to show kindness, I have done with killing, I will have no more of it.

Malachi: If you let them go, there will be quarrels again and killing.

Brian: I think not. They have learned their lesson, they know their master.

Murrough: If you let them go, it is hardly our own army will let them.

Brian: Is it with the threat of an army you are thinking to force me, boy?

Murrough: It is as if you yourself are forcing a peace.

Brian: That is what I am doing and what I have the right to do. I will make an end of quarrels. I will make an end of this custom of death answering to death through the generations, like the clerks answering to one another at the Mass. I will force a peace. Murrough, cut these cords. (*Murrough does so slowly.*)

Malachi: It is against my will you are doing it.

Brian: Are they freed? Give back their arms to these kings.

Malachi: They are no kings now, but traitors that have been worsted.

Brian: I say they are kings.   Maelmora, I give you back your own kingdom of Leinster.   Sitric, I give you your old town of Dublin to keep and to mind, for Ireland and for me.

Malachi: (*Rising.*) This is war then and the breaking of peace.

Brian: It is not, but the beginning of peace.

Malachi: I will raise Connacht against you. I will call to my kinsmen in the north.

Gormleith: You know well you will get no help from the north, or from any other place, against King Brian.

Malachi: That will be known soon and very soon.

Brian: If you think you can keep the High Kingship by force, I will give you the length of a month or of a quarter to bring your men together.

Malachi: A month will be enough.   I will lose no minute.   The north and the west will be against you.   (*He goes out followed by Rury.*)

Brian: War upon us again.   Well, it was laid down—and I am ready.

Gormleith: He will get no help, Brian.   No one at all will come out against you.   His own messenger has said that in a song.   He went east and west, north and south, and he

found the one story in every place. There was
not a man in all Ireland that would raise a
hand against King Brian.

Brian: His own messenger has said that? Then
the sap of power has turned from him to me.
The Man beyond is giving Ireland into my charge!
His right hand is stretched over the north, his
left to the south towards the sun, his face is
towards the west. His angels have set their lad-
der upon Usnach, Victor, angel of Patrick, Axal,
angel of Columcille, Michael, leader of armies!
It is a great thing they are doing for me giving
me the help of their hands. (*Rises.*) Ireland, Ireland, I see you free and high and wealthy; wheat
in every tilled field, beautiful vessels in the houses
of kings, beautiful children well nourished in
every house. No meddling of strangers within
our merings, no outcry of Gael against Gael! It
is not so, Malachi will get help. Why am I
taking the words of a woman, of a song? I have
not done with war. (*Malachi comes back.*)

Murrough: He has come back to ask more time.

Brian: If he is in need of more time, I will
give him up to a year.

Malachi: I have a hard thing to say. I will
not bring destruction on my people. I take back
my big words. The luck has turned against me.
The people have turned from me. I have no help
to get. Queen Gormleith was speaking truth.

Brian: You are saying you will not bring
out your men against us?

Malachi: I will keep them ready, but it will be
against the Gall.

Brian: You will give up all you are claiming.
You will give up that crown?

Malachi: I will not, but I must. (*Takes it off.*)

Brian: God has given me the power, it is to
God I have to answer, it is for the peace of
Ireland I have taken it.

Malachi: (*Giving it.*) Take it and the weight
of it. Yet it was in the prophecy that I would
be king after you in Tara.

Brian: I lift it in my hand that is stronger
than your hand. I will send out the name of this
kingdom through the entire world. I will bring
all Ireland under the one strong rule.

Gormleith: Long life and a good life to Brian,
High King of Ireland!

All (*but Malachi*): Long life to the High King.

Malachi: It is not you, yourself, Brian, have
done this. It may seem to you this queen has
brought you luck doing it. She has turned my
luck backwards. Who is the next she will turn
her hand against?

Gormleith: (*Going on her knees.*) Do not listen
to him, Brian. I would walk the world for you,
and you having showed kindness to my darlings!
You are my master, he never mastered me! In

the time to come whoever may fail you, I myself will never fail or disappoint you!

Brian: (*Lifting her and turning to Brennain.*) Brennain, you need not share these riches. They are little enough altogether to offer to the Queen of Tara.   (*They all turn to look at the spoils.*)

Rury: (*At door.*) The coach is ready, master. The horses are fed and rested.   (*He goes out.*)

Malachi: (*At threshold.*) I will go. I have been long enough in this little place. A little place, a narrow place for so much buying and selling. Great gains, great losses. The crown of Ireland for Brian, the High Kingship for Brian, the treasures of Glenmama for Gormleith. Who has the worst of it? Brian has that Crow of Battle!   (*Goes out.*)

Curtain

Act III

[BEFORE CLONTARF]

Scene: Same room at Kincora. Gormleith sitting in a chair gloomily, her head in her hands. Sitric asleep at back. Maelmora comes in.

Maelmora: Are you so much up in the world at this time, Gormleith, that you will not give me a welcome?

Gormleith: (*Getting up to greet him.*) I did not know you were come. They never told me. Speak easy. Do not waken Sitric, he is only here a short while. He was travelling through the night time from Dublin.

Maelmora: They told me you were here. They said you did not like to be troubled with messengers.

Gormleith: I do not like the messages they bring me, that is all. "Will the Queen come to hear the reading of holy writings?" "Will the Queen come to make ready for saints and bishops?" "Will the

Queen come and kneel to wash the muddy feet
of the poor?"

Maelmora: Brian is surely getting a great name
of piety to put along with his name of riches and
of power; having, as he has, his head in the skies,
and his hand in every good work.

Gormleith: Where is the use of gaining power
if you go turn from it after to shadows? Heaven
may be there as they say, but it is on earth we
are living yet. We cannot stop the work of the
day to go blinking after dreams of the night. And
that is the thing Brian is doing at this time.

Maelmora: If he does, it is that age is coming
upon him as it must come upon us all. What ails
you not to let him travel his own way?

Gormleith: There is no other way to rouse him.
It is laid on me to keep him to the strength and
the power of a king. It is I myself made him
call the whole army together on this day, to do
its exercises that you were bidden to come and
see.

Maelmora: I took notice a long way off of the
tents and the flags and great troops of men. But
what occasion is there for gathering them at this
time more than any other time?

Gormleith: When Brian will see his men that
helped him in his fighting time, it may stir his
mind with the thought of those days, and turn it
to do some great hardy thing.

Maelmora: You had best have left the army
to its rest. There is no peacock can have his tail
spread out ever and always. And mind what I
say, it is a woman's trade to be making all easy
for her comrade the time he has a mind to live
easy. To go rising early, hunting, or fighting, he
is well content to do it, if it is of himself he does
it. But a woman to be rousing him at the calling
of the pigeons to the dawn, and to be drawing
down on him the work he has to do, he will think
her the worst in the world.

Gormleith: I am wishful indeed to be pleasant
to him. He was very good to me. The world
never saw a better man.

Maelmora: Give in to him now and humour
him. If it pleases him to make much of learned
men, let you yourself make more again of them.
If it pleases him to be praying, let you be at hand
to say out the Amen; and believe me you will put
a net about him that will never give way.

Gormleith: Indeed I have striven these many
years to be helpful to him. He used to be uneasy,
not having me at his hand. I lived in his looks
and he in mine.

Maelmora: That is the way it should be.
Let you keep on that road and you will never
go astray.

Gormleith: But now it seems like as if my hold
on him is going from me. His mind is as if slip-

ping away to some place I cannot reach to, that
I do not know.

Maelmora: He is near spun out, and it is right
for him to be attending to his soul. Do not be
grudging him his own comfort in fasting and in
psalms. To be worrying yourself starts wrinkles.
Keep the flowery look in your face and do not
be managing more than your share. Did you
learn yet to put thread in a needle? The clasp
is gone from this cloak. Have you e'er a one
to give me before I will wear it again?

(*Sitric moves and leans on elbow listening.*)

Gormleith: I will put my own clasp on it and
welcome. When was the old one lost?

Maelmora: It was in the journey this morning.
My people and the people of the Desii were bringing the fir trees Brian had sent asking for, and a
dispute arose who should take the lead. I was
not willing there should be any delay, and I put
my own shoulder under one of the trees.

Gormleith: You, my brother, put your shoulder
under a load?

Maelmora: There was no dispute after that
who was to take the lead. But the branch of a
tree caught in the clasp and dragged it, and it
was lost.

Gormleith: You, the King of Leinster, carried
a load of timber into Kincora! I will sew no
clasp upon the cloak.

Maelmora: I saw no shame doing that much for Brian that gave me my liberty and my life.

Gormleith: But I myself see great shame in it. I see you growing dull and soft and gentle, like an old man that would be nearing his end.

Maelmora: Quiet yourself, Gormleith. You were always wild in your young youth, dragging me there and hither from the nurses. You have had the tormenting of three husbands since that time. Leave your brother alone.

Gormleith: I will not give in to it! It is Brian is bringing you to it with the doing away of war. No marching and running and wrestling, but attending on the preaching of the friars. There is not a hound belonging to you dares so much as to follow a hare across the merings, without leave from the judges or the law. You are getting no fair play, closed in here and there, having no liberty in the way you used, to go out fighting for your own profit. I tell you, the time Brian will die from you, he will leave you weak and groping and blind, your hands without strength or readiness, by reason of having slackened from the work. Drowsy you are growing the same as old spent men. The priest sounds the bell, and Brian follows it, and the rest of you follow after Brian.

Maelmora: My poor Queen, I give you up altogether. You were surely born on a Friday, and

the briars breaking through the green sod. Give
me my cloak and I will go where the chess players
are. Murrough called to me from there a while
ago.

Gormleith: I will sew no clasp upon the cloak,
or let you put it on you at all. It is no up-reared
man it is fit for, but a serving man. Let the
fire burn it to ashes, the fire is its fitting place.

> (*She throws it in the fire and Maelmora goes
> out. Sitric rises up and comes for-
> ward.*)

Sitric: That was good talk you were giving out
to Maelmora. It is a queer thing a brother of
your own to be some way sleepy and easy to
satisfy.

Gormleith: I am no way to be blamed for my
brother; but it would be right to put blame on
me, my son to turn sluggish in the same way.
And that is not a likely thing to happen. It is
not my son that is without sap running in him.
It is not a king's son of the Danes will content
himself using meat, or stretched in sleep like a
rich man, or calling out his sins like an old man,
or a man on his last sick bed.

Sitric: I knew well you would give your coun-
tenance to the work I have taken in hand.

Gormleith: What work is that?

Sitric: I am come from joining with my own
people. There was a ship of their ships came to

9

Dublin, bringing presents for Brian, as was said.
The whole of their ships are on their way. It is
given out they are to make an attack upon Wales.
It is not to Wales that they are going. When
the Danes were driven out from here, there was
no one of them gave up the claim to his land
and its ownership. It is to get back their estates
they are coming with their army at this time.

Gormleith: The Danes coming against us?

Sitric: Brian will be left his own estate and
his domain. Never fear, there will no harm happen him. He will be left with the most thing
he cares for, with his churches and with his bells.

Gormleith: The Danes coming back to Ireland!
That is a thing that must not happen! I will not
let it be done! They must be driven back if they
make any attempt to land.

Sitric: It is at Clontarf they are coming to
land. I myself am giving them my help, and I
am expecting your own help.

Gormleith: You are out of your wits thinking
that. You know well I will give you no help.
What you are thinking to do is no less than
treachery.

Sitric: What way were you scolding at Maelmora this very minute, casting up against him
that he was soft and peaceable, clogged with ease,
doing nothing for his own hand? You were jib-
ing at him because he gave in to Brian's law. I

have my mind made up to break away from it, and you are no better content with myself. You know well you were calling out this good while, that nothing would serve the country but some war.

Gormleith: I tell you I will not let treachery be used by any one that is belonging to me. If I called for war, I did not call to you to bring it, but to leave it to the chances of the times.

Sitric: If you had not led me to make sure of your help, why would I have promised it to Sigurd Earl of Orkney and to Brodar of the Isle of Man?

Gormleith: You promised them that?

Sitric: They asked a promise. Sigurd would not come join us without your call, he wrote his asking in this letter. Brodar wrote an asking of his own—there are the letters, you have to put your name to them. We have not so good a chance without having Brodar and Sigurd at our back.

Gormleith: (*Reading letters.*) What daring they have, writing that! What sort are they thinking me to be? I will send them no answer at all. I will go and tell out the whole case to Brian. Let Brian himself send the answer.

Sitric: Do so, and make ready a sheet for my burying. It is known I have been speaking with the messengers of the Danes. I am surely dead,

or as good as dead, you making Brian uneasy
and questioning.

Gormleith: Hurry, hurry then, go away out of
this! I will not tell him until such time as you
are safe. Make no delay! I must give the warning. He must lead his army to protect Clontarf.
Go, hurry, make yourself safe.

Sitric: Where would I go to? In what place
would I be safe? Is it in Brian's country, hunted
as an outlaw? Or with the Danes, telling them I
had broken my promise and my word? I have
no mind to go wandering, hiding in bushes and
under rocks.

Gormleith: I will send you word if Brian goes
against you—I will not let any harm fall on you.
Go, now go.

Sitric: I will not quit this place, until such time
as your name is put to this letter and to that.

Gormleith: You are talking madness. That
would be a treason out of measure! I am bound
to Brian. I will be faithful to Brian. I am well
pleased I turned against Malachi. I will never
fail Brian or disappoint him.

Brennain: (*At door.*) The High King is coming here, Queen, to take a view of the army
from the door.

Sitric: You have leave to give me up to him.
I am well rewarded for taking heed to a woman's
words. It is only a fool would pay attention to

big words from any woman at all. Queen or no queen she will turn timorous, and run and fail you at the last.

Brian: (*Coming in.*) You are welcome here, Sitric. Did you bring any strange news from Dublin? They were telling me you had calling on you some messengers of the Danes.

Sitric: A ship that called to me with payments. They have sent back at your order the golden vessels and the painted books that were stolen from the churches in the time gone by. There are here a couple of the books. The vessels are weighty, they are at the door below. (*Shows books.*)

Brian: I am well pleased to get them. I would not wish those holy vessels to be left in any heathen hands. Go, Sitric, give them into the hands of the priests to be put in the chapel before the vespers will ring. I will call to the Bishops to consecrate them, coming back to the service of Christ.

Sitric: The ship having left them, sailed away.
(*Goes.*)

Brian: Take notice, Queen, that the men of the army have been gathered together according to your desire.

Gormleith: (*At window.*) I was looking at them a while ago. The hillsides are speckled with the troops of them.

Brian: (*Sitting down.*)   It is a comfortable thought it is only for show and for pleasure they are come.   We have nothing to go out fighting for any more.

Brennain: That is so, that is so, what need is there for fighting?   Men of all learning struggling at the door, seven kings' messengers asking our friendship, a hundred cooks dressing the dinner, a tun of wine offered us for every day in the year.   We will have to widen the whole world to hold Ireland, and to widen Ireland itself to hold Kincora!

Gormleith: (*Turning to Brian.*)   Come and look from the window.   You can see a great throng of your men.

Brian: I think the time is come when I can let them all scatter to their own districts.

Gormleith: We have work for them to do together yet.

Brian: Their best work would be to put a thatch to their houses, and to turn all the wild scrub to barley gardens.   What did the wandering woman say?   To bring down Adam's Paradise again.   I had some dream in the night time, it has gone from me—some dream of a place where war was not remembered.

Gormleith: It is best to keep our men to the work they are trained for, that is fighting.

Brian: I have made Ireland safe.   I have put

her name up among the nations. I have put on
her the three crowns, the crown of wheat for
strength, the crown of apples for pleasantness,
the crown of lasting peace. I will break up
the army for a year and a day. I will leave
every man time to forgive his enemies, and to
make his own settlement with God.

Gormleith: (*Coming to Brian.*) You would
make a great mistake doing that. I give you
a strong advice to keep the army at its full
strength. Believe me I am not without reason
saying that.

Brian: Has there any news come to you of
danger?

Gormleith: News, news, it is nothing new I
am saying. Ireland has been fighting these ten
thousand years, and that custom to be changed,
it is likely she would go to nothing. Peace, the
priests have their tongues framed to it, peace,
peace, peace. Is it certain it is so good a thing?
Some that know all might not say that. It is
in the sluggish time the little men grow to be
many, and the great men give up living, and the
trader has the sway. It is not you yourself
would be satisfied, seeing that time to come.

Brian: I will be satisfied and well satisfied the
time I will have shaped everything that is under
me to the will of God. There is no fighting in
that good place the Almighty has of his own.

Gormleith: This is the world and you cannot change the world's old custom. There must be fighting so long as there is anything at all worth fighting for. If there was not war in the world it would be right to make a war, to search out something to hate. Yes, I know all the talk of love and charity, but it is not of malice I am talking, but of the fury of a blast of wind against a heap of rotten dust. Keep your army ready to your hand now. Have you never a mind to go forcing the Cross on the nations of the East? Armenia, where the Holy Tree was put up, is owned now by heathens that deny it. Other uses to fail, that would be a great thing and a grand thing for your army to do.

Brian: If I had a score less of years upon me, that would be a good thing to do. But the time fails me, and I have no leave to do but the one thing. I have leave in my own narrow kingdom to begin the thousand years of peace.

Gormleith: Maybe some danger may rise up. We are never done with danger. Suppose now the Danes should come attacking, striving to win back what they have lost.

Brian: That is a thing will not happen.

Gormleith: They are coveting to get back their old estates—they will not give up what they owned so readily as you may think. They might send out a fleet of ships—they might make it out

to be going to some other place—they might
gather other leaders to their help. When all
would seem safe and quiet, just as it does this
day, they might come to land suddenly—giving
no warning. Let you keep your men ready for
that.

Brian: Sitric has but just come from seeing
their messengers and speaking with them. He
has the whole strand in his charge, he would
know if there was any thought of an attack.
There is no fear of the Danes.

Gormleith: Yes, yes, Sitric would know—
then they cannot be coming. But the provinces?
You said you would not take your hand from the
work till you had made all quiet in the provinces.
There is a stir in them. They are starting up
against you here and there. They are going
back to their lawless ways. There is a king of
Burren wanting to force a rent on Galway.
There are uproars and robberies in the north.

Brian: That is bad news, but it may not be
true, it may have grown in the telling. Are
you very certain it is true?

Gormleith: I am certain.

Brian: I am sorry indeed to hear that. I
thought the very day had come when I could
free myself from this (*touches sword*) altogether.
But that hope was a deceit and a flattery.

Gormleith: Come out now and consult with

the captains. Bid them make themselves ready
to go and put down all these troubles.

Brian: If there is trouble to be put down I
myself will go and do it. I will not slacken my
hand so long as there is work to be done. But
my heart is tired out with waiting for the keening and the treachery to be at an end.

Gormleith: Come out, come out before the door.
They will give you a great welcome there.

(*They are going to door when Brennain
appears in it.*)

Brennain: There is some one here that is
asking to see the King.

Gormleith: The King cannot see any person
at all at this time.

Brian: Who is it is wanting me?

Brennain: The travelling woman was here a
long time ago—she has the appearance of one that
would be wasted and worn with the length of the
road.

Brian: Bid her to come in. (*Brennain turns
and lifts hand, Beggar comes in.*)

Beggar: It is many long days since I saw you
before, King Brian.

Brian: What have you been going through in
all that time?

Beggar: Going on my two feet, tramping fro
and hither, looking for the news would free you
to sit down at the table of the angels.

Brian: Christ knows well I would hurry to that supper, and I being free to attend it. But I am hindered here and there. At this time the trouble and the disturbance is in the provinces of Ireland.

Beggar: There is no disturbance and no trouble.

Brian: What way can you know that?

Beggar: (*Holding up ring.*) Are you remembering the ring you gave me? There it is before you. I had to hide it for a good while, the time of quiet was not come. But at the last I have walked the whole country, and I lifting it up in my hand.

Brian: Did you go with yourself only, without company?

Beggar: Through the five provinces I went, from this to Toraigh in the north and from that again to Cliona's wave in the south, with no one but myself and the goodness of the Lord.

Brian: Did no one meddle with you?

Beggar: When I was passing through Connacht there were young men riding horses, and they came as if at me. But then they said: "We will leave her free seeing we ourselves are free and all Ireland is free."

Brennain: That is good, that is good. If Connacht is quiet all Ireland is quiet.

Beggar: When I went down into the north I

took notice of a troop of rough men and one of
them said: "It is no harm to rob this girl that is
of the province of Munster." But another man
of them said: "Do not, for it is not to the north or
the south we belong now, but to the whole of
Ireland." And for the peace of the whole country,
King Brian, they thank God and you.

Brian: That is a lucky journey you have
made, and a great story you have brought me.
Many a woman has sat beside a king through
her lifetime, and has done less than that to
be remembered by.

Beggar: You can put away your sword this
time, and turn your face entirely towards Heaven.

Gormleith: The King has work to do yet.
His life has not run to its end.

Beggar: You are out of it, Queen, his life is
near its beginning—the beginning of the lasting
life of Heaven.

Gormleith: You do well preaching quiet, and
your own heart so uneasy. You run here and
run there, changing and vanishing like the moon.

Beggar: I run towards my home that is in
the place beyond. I will take my rest when
I have reached my home. Now I will go, I
have given my message to the King.

Brian: It is a great message you have carried. It is from beyond the world it is come.
This great new peace was made for me beyond

the world. I saw it in a vision of the night. It is your voice is calling it back to me.

Beggar: It is likely it was the one message sent by some other messenger.

Brian: I saw in my dream a woman coming to me, many coloured, changing, that was Aoibhell the friend of my race. She came and she called to me and swept the darkness away, and showed me the whole country, shining and beautiful, an image of the face of God in the smooth sea. All bad things had gone from it like plover to the north at the strengthening of the sun. The rowan berries on Slieve Echtge were the lasting fruits of Heaven. The Gael had grown to be fitting comrades for the white angels. I could hear the joyful singing of the birds of the Land of Promise.

Beggar: That was a good vision and a very good dream. Those that hear that music will never be satisfied in any place where it is not found.

Brian: It went from me then, and I cried out after it, but Aoibhell said: "It is only at Clontarf you will come again to that vision and that perfect peace."

Beggar: Why did she say Clontarf? I wonder what meaning she had in that.

Brian: It is often dreams have not a straight meaning, or waking breaks it. It is here at Kin-

cora I have had a witness to the perfect peace
and not at Clontarf.   Now, now at last I can
put away my sword!

Beggar: Give it here to me.   Give me that
sword, I will hang it here upon the wall.   (*He
gives it and she hangs it up.*)

Gormleith: Has the army that is outside gone
from your mind?

Brian: I am going out to it now, it is the last
time I will have need of it.   I will set every
man of them free after the supper, that will be
the feast of God's peace.

Gormleith: I ask of you, Brian, and I beg and
I pray you to give in to what I say.   I came
here to put your name up, to bring you luck.
I turned every stone for you, you will lose
your name, you will lose me, oh, what can I
say to turn you?

Brian: Have I and time not quieted this
whirling heart?   Go get yourself ready for the
supper.   Put on your silks and your jewels to
do honour to it, your eyes are shining, they
will shine out at the feast.

Beggar: Come, Brian, to the supper of the
angels.   To the Garden of Paradise and the
branchy Tree of Life.

Gormleith: Go away, woman, out of this!   He
would listen to what would save him, and you
not meddling!   You are putting spells of weak-

ness on him with your hymns. Do not let her
entice you, Brian! Do not listen to that travelling woman of the roads, that tattered moon-
mad beggar.

Brian: It is not her voice is calling to me but
the voices from the place beyond.

Beggar: (*At door.*)
Gabriel, the Virgin's messenger, is come,
Michael, the rider of the speckled horse, is
     come.
Axal, the good steerer, Rafael of our love
Giving out the blessing for the supper of the
     King.

Gormleith: Go then, go, go to your destruction, drag the King to his destruction, let him
go his own way! I do not begrudge it to him or
to you. I tried to save him. He would not
listen. He has made his choice, I am not in
fault! The curse of Ireland be upon all beggars
and their meddlings!

Brian: (*Turning back in doorway.*) Go, Gormleith, to the church and pray, bend your knees,
pray and repent, pray and repent, till the wildness has gone from your eyes and the pride
from your heart, and the darkness from your
vexed unhappy mind. (*He goes out.*)

Gormleith: Go then, go, I have done all
I can do. I have done. I have no place and no
part in you! I have not, I have not, I am

done with Kincora. (*She throws herself in chair tearing her handkerchief in her rage. Maelmora and Sitric come in.*)

Maelmora: We thought Brian was with you.

Gormleith: What brings you back here? Have you no more loads to carry? Why are you not carrying firing for the priests that have mastered your High King?

Maelmora: This is a good welcome I am getting this day. Insults from you and insults from Murrough.

Gormleith: What did you do to anger your master's son?

Sitric: He was watching Murrough at the chess and he gave an advice, and Murrough followed it and lost the game. Murrough was angry then.

Maelmora: I would not stop to listen to him. He has no right to put insults on me.

Gormleith: He had a right to do it. You give in to a master that gives in to monks and beggars. It is certain you and Ireland were never under disgrace till now.

Sitric: You will sign these letters now, I think, that you would not sign a while ago.

Gormleith: I will—I will! Give them to me quickly. He made little of me. He will be sorry. He bid me go and pray, he bid me repent. I

will not, it is he himself will be made repent!
(Takes up pen.)

Maelmora: What is it you are doing?

Gormleith: I am breaking away from Brian,
I am breaking Brian's peace.

Maelmora: You, his wife?

Gormleith: It was to a great king I came as
a wife, not to a monkish man serving heaven on
his knees.

Maelmora: (*Holding her hand.*) You must
not go against him.—He that gave you all.

Gormleith: He has taken all away that was
worth having.

Sitric: Let her sign.

Maelmora: This is no less than treachery.

Gormleith: Go and call your king, so, and give
me up to him. (*She signs.*) Send the letters,
Sitric, I am ready to go. (*Gets up.*)

Maelmora: Where are you going?

Gormleith: To welcome the foreign armies that
are on the sea now coming to Ireland.

Maelmora: You must not do it! I will not
let you be a traitor in this house.

Gormleith: Be a king again, Maelmora; join
with us and fight in the old way. You yourself
and Sitric could keep Ireland against all the world.

Maelmora: I will call out to Brian.

Gormleith: You need not call to him. Here
is Murrough his son, give us up to him, humble

10

us before him. Humble yourself before him, and let the son of the Connacht woman put bonds upon me and on my son.

(*Murrough comes in. Sitric goes out quickly, hiding the letters.*)

Murrough: Are you giving advice to the Queen, Maelmora, as you gave it to me a while ago? I am ashamed that you vexed me then, but she seems twenty times more vexed.

Maelmora: It is the Queen that is giving advice to me. It may be better for you if I do not take it.

Murrough: I am no good at guessing riddles. But if there is some threat in your voice I will answer it.

Maelmora: Have a care now. You may thank the four bones of your father I did not answer you a while ago.

Gormleith: What was it he said to vex you?

Murrough: I said the King of Leinster was well able to give advice. I said it was good advice he gave his comrades, the Danes, the day they ran from us like scared sheep at Glenmama.

Maelmora: It may happen us yet to meet in another battle, where it is not my men but your own men that will run like scattered sheep.

Murrough: When that battle is at hand, King, see that there is a good yew-tree near by, a tree where you can hide while your men are running as you hid yourself at Glenmama.

Maelmora: (*Half drawing sword.*) I will not lay a hand on you in this house; my answer will be in some place of battle.

Murrough: That answering will not be sooner than I wish it.

Gormleith: Its day will come sooner than you think.

Murrough: No, our ill-wishers do not come out against us now, they only plot and plan.

Gormleith: They are coming out now. They are coming to make their attack on you.

Murrough: I do not think so; they are afraid.

Gormleith: No, they are not afraid; you will not stand against them this time. They will sweep you and your race out of Ireland.

Murrough: Where are these great men coming from? Will the grass stalks turn to be an army?

Gormleith: I am giving you a last warning. They are on the sea now. The north wind is bringing them to Clontarf.

Murrough: That is the foolish talk of women in a parlour. Sitric would bring his men out from Dublin, they would have a rough landing at Clontarf. Where is Sitric? He has stolen away. Where is he gone?

Gormleith: Sitric is young, he is hardy; he would not sit down and count his beads through his life. The old have worn out their time, from this out is it for you and Sitric to strike the ball.

Maelmora: This is no place for us now. Come away, Gormleith, out of this.

Murrough: (*Standing at the door.*) No one must leave this till the King comes. (*Calls out.*) Here, men, call in the King—hurry, there is trouble before him—tell him to make no delay.

Gormleith: I would not have crept out of the house secretly. I will tell him myself what I have done.

Murrough: You will not tell him of your treachery, and I that am not your friend will not tell him. I have no mind to scald my father's heart.

Brian: (*Coming in.*) What is this call of trouble?

Murrough: The armies of the Gall are on their way to Ireland.

Brian: Are you sure of what you say?

Murrough: I have it from those that know. It is certain.

Brian: The army is ready, we are well prepared. Call in our advisers; I will see what is best to do. Come here to me, Gormleith, it is your hour now, you are very wary in giving advice and very brave in danger. Stay here beside me now while we make our plans.

Gormleith: I cannot—I do not know what to

say—you made me angry. You must not trust
me.

Brian: My heart has trusted you since we
were linked in marriage, many long days ago.
Sit here as you used—take that pen and mark
down the orders for our troops. (*Takes pen
and gives it to her.*)

Gormleith: (*Throwing it from her.*) I cannot—
oh, it must be stopped—they must be turned
back—it is not too late—help me, Maelmora,
Sitric must do as I bid him. Call him back
—go after him, he must obey me—no, I will
go myself. I will drag him back. Yes, Brian,
you may trust me—I will stop him, everything
will turn out well. (*She is going to the door
when Malachi appears in it.*) Who is that?
Malachi!

Malachi: (*Putting up his hand.*) Stop where
you are. I have a thing to say to the High
King.

Gormleith: Oh, are you come for my destruction at the last?

Malachi: I have heavy news for you, Brian.
There is danger on its way towards us.

Brian: I got news of it on the minute. You
are in time to help us. We are on the one side,
we have had such dangers before this.

Malachi: Are you very sure there are no
traitors here to make our enemies welcome?

Brian: There should surely be some weighty reason urging you to give out such a word.

Malachi: I would sooner some other one would ask, is there treachery within the very lintel of this door?

Brian: Maelmora, have you any answer to give to that?

Maelmora: The time Murrough called to you, it was to tell what I was after telling him.

Brian: Murrough would not screen any traitor at all, whoever it might happen to be.

Murrough: Maelmora is in it—and——

Brian: And what other one?

Murrough: I am loth to say it. It is best for you to question her yourself.

Brian: Question her? Who is there to question? There is no woman here but the Queen.

Gormleith: Make an end of it, Murrough. Tell out what he is asking you to tell.

Murrough: Queen Gormleith is giving her own welcome to the Danes.

Brian: That is not possible, that is some great mistake. Tell him, Gormleith, it is a mistake and a lie.

Gormleith: He has told you no lie. The thing he has said is true.

Brian: It is not true. You are taking this thing on your own head with some thought of saving your son.

Gormleith: Ask King Malachi. He knows me, he made prophecies, he will tell you. I would sooner you to know the truth, and the end to have come and the finish. Tell it out, Malachi, I make no defence, and tell him along with that what wages are my due.

Malachi: I am done with giving judgments this long time. It is God is the rightful judge.

Gormleith: I did it and I did not do it, Brian— I was not entirely to blame. I thought myself to be wise, to drag things here and there, to do some great thing, moving men with big words. Oh, I have pulled down the rafters of the roof that sheltered me! (*She is putting out her hand to Brian but Malachi goes between.*)

Brian: Let her go, let no one lay a hand on her. And may God have mercy on every woman's vain changing heart!

Gormleith: Do not say that, Brian, do not think it, it was not my heart that changed, it was anger and jealousy made me crazy at the time.

(*Brian's head has sunk in his hands. Malachi gently leads her towards the door.*)

Malachi: Go now as he has given you leave. Go free, if freedom can profit you, a broken woman, a spoiled queen, travelling the roads of the world. God is the judge. You were maybe

misled, made use of, others putting it on you
that you yourself were doing all.

Gormleith: No, Malachi, I did my own part,
I have no mind to deny or to hide my own
share in it at all. You promised Brian I would
turn my hand against him, and I thought that a
thing was not possible, and I did turn it against
him in the end. Listen now to this. Brodar of
Manannan's Island would not give his aid to
the Danes unless I promised him myself, and I
promised it. I put my own hand to that. Sigurd,
Earl of Orkney, asked the same promise, and I
gave it. I did not leave any lie on you at all
—your words have come around. There will be
fighting for me yet! Fighting for me and about
me. Are you satisfied now, Malachi of the
foretellings?

Malachi: Look at the work you have done.
(*He points to Brian.*) Go out and hang your
head for shame. The man that was steady and
strong is broken. It is hardly he will reach to the
battle.

Gormleith: No fear, no fear, Brian will reach
to the battle. There is no fear at all of him
not doing that. It is not Brian would wish to
die the death of a man that is lessening and stiff-
ening, the time he grows attentive to his bed,
but of a winner that is merry and shouting, the
time his enemies are put down. I was maybe

a right wife for him. A right wife, a lucky wife, in spite of all! (*Goes out.*)

Malachi: (*Going to Brian and putting hand on his shoulder.*) Lift up your head, Brian.

Brian: The blame is on me. It is I myself have betrayed my people. War, war, keening and treachery, Ireland red again, red and stained through and through—trouble and treachery and war.

Malachi: Make ready your orders for the army.

Brian: Is all ready for the Queen's journey? Give her the horses from Connacht.

Malachi: Listen to what I say, we must send messengers.

Brian: The speckled horses, she liked them best, and the carved chariot from the north.

Malachi: Attend to what I am saying.

Brian: But who was it, who was it, that called in the Gall?

Malachi: I cannot rouse him. It is no wonder. That treachery was too hard a blow.

> (*Murrough comes in with standard in hand and stands on threshold. Spears and banners appear at window. War march is played.*)

Brian: (*Standing up.*) But what did the dream mean? What did Aoibhell mean? She promised me lasting peace, lasting peace; she told it to me

in my dream.   (*He walks towards door.*)   What
did she mean?   Is there no truth?   Is every one
treacherous?   (*He comes face to face with Murrough
and stands still.*)

Murrough: The army is ready, we must lead
it to meet the Danes at Clontarf.

Brian: (*Standing very strong and straight.*)
Clontarf?   Now I know what Aoibhell meant.
She said it was at Clontarf I would find peace.
That is well.   My place is ready among the
generations; Cathal, son of Aedh, Corc, son of
Anluan, Lorcan, son of Luchta, Mahon, son of
Cennedigh, all the race of Lugaidh reigned in this
place, and went out of this door for the last time;
and the traitors that betrayed them, and the
women they loved.   Give me my sword.   (*Malachi
takes it down and gives it to him.*)   It has another
battle to win.

Curtain

DERVORGILLA

PERSONS

Dervorgilla . . ONCE QUEEN OF BREFFNY
Flann . . . . . AN OLD SERVANT
Mona . . . . . . HIS WIFE
Owen . . . . . . A YOUNG MAN
Other Young Men
Mamie . . . . A GIRL
Other Girls
A Wandering Songmaker

Time — 1193. Scene, outside the Abbey of Mellifont, near Drogheda.

*Scene : A green lawn outside a garden wall.
Flann is arranging a chair with cloaks and
cushions. Mona standing beside him.*

Mona: Put a cloak there on the ground, Flann.
It would not serve the lady, the damp of the
earth to be rising up about her feet.

Flann: What ails her coming abroad at all,
and the length of time she never asked to come
outside the walls?

Mona: The young lads wanting to get prizes
and to show off at their sports, it is that enticed
her entirely. More sports there will be in it to-day
than the most of them saw in their lifetime.

Flann: Fighting and killings and robbery, that
is the sport they were brought up to, and that is
all the sport that was in it for the last twoscore
years.

Mona: The Lord be with the good old times,
when a woman suckling her child would be safe
crossing Ireland from sea to sea! No wonder our
own poor lady to be vexed and torn in the night-
time. It seemed to me she had a very shook
appearance this morning.

Flann: There is no occasion for her to be fretting or lonesome, and the way her name is up through the whole of the province.

Mona: Why would n't it be up, after the way she fed old and young through the bad times, giving means and cattle to those the English had robbed.

Flann: It is royal she is in giving as in race. Look at all the weight of gold the Abbey got from her, and the golden vessels upon the high altar.

Mona: No wonder the people to be saying she will surely get the name of a saint; the darling queen-woman of the Abbey of Mellifont.

Flann: God grant it, God grant it. We have her secret well kept so far as this. It would be a queer thing if it would not be kept to the end.

(*Shouts are heard.*)

Mona: It is the lads shouting for their own champions that are after beating the men of Assaroe.

(*Owen and other lads come in.*)

Owen: Is the lady herself coming out, Flann? Has she got good prizes in her hand?

Flann: Good and too good. The lady is too much bothered with the whole of you, stretching out her hand to you the way she does.

Another lad: Show us the prizes.

Another lad: Are they there in the basket, Flann? Give them over here to me.

Flann: Let you behave yourselves now and have manners, or you will get nothing at all.

Owen: It is little we would get if you had the giving of it, Flann! Here, Mamie, come and see the grand things Flann is keeping under his cloak!

(*They all hustle Flann. Mamie runs in.*)

Mamie: Do you see what is there beyond? Beyond upon the hill?

Owen: A troop of men on horses. I suppose it is to race the horses they are come.

Mamie: It is not, it is not; but a troop of English soldiers they are. Bows they have and swords. I am in dread of them. I went hiding in the scrub as they passed. Is there any fear, Flann, they will be coming to this place?

Flann: Sure the lady herself is coming outside the gate. Would I let her do that, there to be danger in it? I tell you the place she is, is as safe as a burrow under rocks.

Mona: Let you stop your chat. Here she is now, coming to the gate.

Mamie: I would never be in dread where she is. There are some say she has power from beyond the world, for there is no one knows her name or her race.

Flann: Whisht, the whole of ye!

(*They stand back and Dervorgilla comes in leaning upon her stick. Flann and*

*Mona lead her to her chair and she
stands for a moment.*)

Dervorgilla: God save you, children.

All: God save you, lady.

Dervorgilla: His blessing be upon you, and my
blessing, and the blessing of the summer time.
Let me see that the doings of the great men are
not forgotten, and that you can be as good
runners, and as good hurlers, and as good at
hitting the mark, as your old fathers were.

All: We will, we will.

Owen: You will be proud, lady, to see
what the men of Ulster can do against the men
of Leinster and of Meath.

Dervorgilla: That is so, I will be proud. For
though I am an old woman given to praying,
I can take pride yet in strength of body and
readiness of hand; for I saw such things long
ago in kings' houses.

Owen: There is no fear of us at all! We will
not be put down; we will gain the day! Come
on, lads, some of the sports might be over. Come
along, Mamie, and be looking at us from the
bank of the embroiderers. (*They go out.*)

Dervorgilla: It is many years since we had
a day like this of sport and of mirth-making. It
seems as if those were wrong who said the
English would always bring trouble on us; there
may be a good end to the story after all.

Flann: There will be a good end, to be sure. A bad behaved race the people of this country are. It is the strong hand of the English is the best thing to be over them.

Dervorgilla: England is a rich, powerful country to be joined to.

Flann: We should surely grow rich ourselves joined with her, the same as a girl of the ducks and the ashes that would be married to a great lord's son.

Dervorgilla: I can go in peace if I know I have left peace after me, and content, but sometimes I am afraid. I had a dream last night, a troublesome dream— What is that? I hear a cry.

(*Mamie runs in with a dead bird.*)

Mamie: Oh, look, lady, it is a crane. It is dead, they have shot it!

Dervorgilla: The fowlers should have spared all life on a day of mirth like this.

Mamie: It was one of the English bowmen; he shot it in the air. It fell at my feet. It died there at my feet.

Dervorgilla: It vexes me, that to have happened on such a day as this.

Flann: Get out of that now, Mamie. You should have more sense than to be bringing in a thing of the kind. Look now, there has blood dropped upon the lady's cloak. Bring it out of this and throw it in some place where it will be in no one's way. I wonder at you annoying the lady, and the way she is spending her means upon you all. (*Mamie goes out.*)

Dervorgilla: (*Looking at cloak which Mona is wiping.*) It has brought to my mind other blood that was spilled, and that I, I myself, have to answer for.

Flann: You think entirely too much of it, lady, taking on yourself the weight of the bringing in of the English. It was the quarrelling of the provinces with one another brought them in.

Dervorgilla: No, no. It was I brought them in for good or for evil, by my own sin and the wars that were stirred up for my sake.

Flann: No, but it was in the prophecies that they would come. Did n't Blessed Caillen see them coming over the sea, and he at the brink of death waiting for the angels of God? There is no use at all trying to go against the prophecies.

Dervorgilla: You are always trying to flatter and to comfort me, but surely I brought trouble upon Ireland, as well as on all I had to do with. Diarmuid, King of Leinster, that was my lover, perished like a beast fallen by the roadside, without sacrament, without repentance. It was I brought that curse upon him.

Flann: (*Mutters.*) It was he himself earned that curse; God knows he earned it well.

Dervorgilla: Was it not I brought the curse upon

O'Rourke, King of Breffny, the husband I left
and betrayed? The head I made bow with shame
was struck off and sent to the English King.
The body I forsook was hung on the walls
shamefully, by the feet, like a calf after slaughter.
It is certain there is a curse on all that have
to do with me. What I have done can never
be undone. How can I be certain of the forgiveness of God?

Mona: Be easy now. Who would be forgiven
if you would not be forgiven? Sure the Lord has
seen your prayers and your crying, and your great
giving and your holy life.

Dervorgilla: Four years I have lived and four-
score, and for half my life I ran my own way,
and through the other half of my life I have paid
the penalty. For every day or night of pride or
of pleasure, I have spent a day and a night of
prayer and of pain. Will not that bring forgiveness? Is not that paying the penalty?

Mona: Indeed and surely you have made it
up with God. Surely you are forgiven and well
forgiven! It is God Himself will open to you
the gate of heaven!

Dervorgilla: But the people, the people; will
they ever forgive what I have done!

Mona: They have enough to do to be mind-
ing themselves. What call would they have to
go draw it down upon you at all?

Dervorgilla: I dreamt last night that the people knew me, that they knew my story and my sin; that they knew it was for my sake the wars were stirred up and the Gall brought into Ireland. They seemed to curse and to threaten me. They stooped like this, to take up stones to throw at me, knowing me at last to be Dervorgilla!

(*A voice is heard singing.*)

Mona: Whist! Listen.

Dervorgilla: What is that? Who is that coming?

Flann: A beggar—some wandering lad. He has a great appearance of poverty. Will I go get something for him? There is no comfort at all comforts you like giving to the poor. Look now the way his shoes are broken!

Dervorgilla: I can help the poor still. God gives me leave to do that. Thank God I have leave yet to be a giver of gifts. Go bring me shoes for him, and a cloak, and some silver money.

Flann: Where is the use spoiling him with silver? Shoes are enough, shoes are enough. What call has a lad of his age to go begging; that is a trade of life should be left to give employment to the old.

(*He goes out. A ragged lad comes in. He is carrying a sort of rough fiddle.*)

Dervorgilla: Where do you come from, boy?

Songmaker: From the province of Connacht

I am come. Connacht yesterday, Armagh to-morrow. To-day it is Mellifont has got hold of me. (*Sings*)—

> Yesterday travelling Connacht,
> Drogheda has me to-day;
> My back to the empty pockets,
> My face to the place will pay!

Dervorgilla: You are young to be wandering.
Songmaker: Where would I be stopping? This day five year the thatch I was reared under was burned by the Gall, and all I had of kindred scattered. I rambled Ireland since that time, just roving around. (*Sings*)—

> Just roving around
> To my grief and my sorrow,
> Under a rock to-day,
> Under a bush to-morrow.

It will be a long time till the Pope of Rome will get a hearth tax on my account, from the tax-gatherers of the King of England.

Dervorgilla: Have you no trade that you can follow?
Songmaker: The best, the best. I have in me the makings of a poet—and a good poet—according to the treatment I would be given—one day sweet, another day sour. (*Sings*)—

Syrupy sweet to-day,
　Sour as sloes to-morrow;
Sweet to the lads that pay,
　Sour to the lads that borrow!

It is a sweet poem I would wish to be making in this grand place.

Dervorgilla: You have no right to the name of a poet; you have not learned it in the schools.

Songmaker: I did learn it well. Was n't my grandfather a poet, and I reared up by him on the brink of a running stream? I know the rules well. Believe me, the mensuration of verses is a very ticklish thing.

Dervorgilla: The old poets had knowledge from the well of wisdom. They could tell and foretell many things.

Songmaker: It is often the people far and near would draw to my grandfather to question him. Let them come to him, sick or sour, he had an answer for all of them, or a cure.

Dervorgilla: Did you ever hear him say to any one that asked him, if a sin once committed could be forgiven?

Songmaker: It wants no poet's knowledge to know that. Can a sin be forgiven, is it? Why not, or who would people heaven?

Dervorgilla: But—did you ever hear him say if it can be undone? Can a wrong once done

ever be undone?   Suppose there was some person
who had done a great wrong, had brought, maybe,
a bad neighbour into the house, or a hard stranger
in among kindred—it might be a race, an army
into a country.   Could that person ever gain
forgiveness, praying and sorrowing?

Songmaker: Well, God is good.   But to bring
in a bad neighbour is a hard thing to get over.   It
was a bad neighbour in the next house, drove St.
Patrick back from Rome to Ireland.

Dervorgilla: But if that neighbour, that
stranger, that race, should turn kind and honest,
or could be sent back, and all be as before, would
not forgiveness be gained by that?

Songmaker: Wait, now, till I think.   There
was something my grandfather, God rest his soul,
used to be saying.   He had great wisdom, I tell
you, being silly-like, and blind.   Wait, now, till
I see can I sound it out right.   Talking, the
neighbours were, about St. Martin's mitten.   It
was St. Martin made a throw of his mitten at
the mice one time they had him annoyed, nib-
bling at the oatenmeal in the mill; and, in the
throwing, it turned to be a cat, and scattered
them.   That was the first cat that ever was in
Ireland.

Mona: To be sure; to be sure; so it was.   St.
Martin's mitten was the first cat.   Everybody
knows that.

Songmaker: But it is what my grandfather
said, that if all the saints in Ireland had wished
it, and if St. Martin himself had wished it
along with them, it would fail them to have
turned that cat to be a mitten again, or the
English to be quiet neighbours again, furry and
innocent, and having no claws!

Flann: (*Bringing cloak and shoes.*) Give
thanks now to the lady that is giving you more
than you deserve. (*Hands him the things and
some money.*)

Songmaker: My blessing down upon you, lady,
whoever you are. Faith, you have a strong
pocket! The house you are in is no empty house,
or any bad house at all. (*He sits down on the
ground and begins to lace on shoes, singing:*)

I am after being given two grand steppers,
   Matching one another like two swallows on
      the wind,
Made from the skin of the Brown Bull of
      Cuailgne.
   Or the cow Argus minded, he that was not
      blind.

It's the roads of the world will be proud to see
      them,
   It's a great ornament they will be, far and
      near;

She that gave them never learned to be a
    niggard,
Though the Gall are among us this four
    and twenty year!
      (*Owen, Mamie, and the rest run in.*)

Owen: I have the prize won! I was best over
the leaps. I have taken the sway!

Mamie: My worked border was the best!
Every one gave in to that!

Another Lad: I leaped very high; I leaped as
high as that!

Another: It was I won at the hurley! I
took the goal from the men of Meath!

Dervorgilla: You have all done well. I am
proud of you, children. I can give you all prizes.
Flann, give me the prizes. (*He hands them to
her and she gives them one by one.*) Here, Mamie,
is a necklace from the Eastern world. You
have earned it well by your worked border.
Make the borders of your house beautiful. Keep
within its borders all God has given you in
charge. (*To Owen.*) Here is a silver cup. (*To
another.*) Here is a cloak with a brooch. (*To
another.*) Here, you are the youngest, you must
have a prize. Take this hurl, this silver ball.
Practice with them well and you will be first yet.
(*They all stoop and kiss her hand as she gives
the presents.*)

Flann: Give a good shout now for the lady. (*They all shout, the singer joins.*)

Owen: Who is that? A stranger? He has not the look of our own people. Is he come to make sport for us?

Dervorgilla: He is a maker of songs. He has the sweet voice of the Connacht men. They have the soft sea mist in their mouths.

Owen: Give out a song now, till we'll hear what you can do.

Songmaker: Give me the key so. There can be no singing without a key.

Owen: What do you call a key?

Songmaker: Three keys there are; you should know that. It is only love or drink or friendship can unlock a song.

Dervorgilla: Give him a cup of wine.

Flann: Will nothing do him but wine? Wine that is too good and too strong. (*Gives him a cup, Songmaker drinks.*)

Songmaker: What will you have now for a song? Destructions, cattle preys, courtships, feats of battle?

Owen: No, no; we are tired of those.

Songmaker: Well, I'll rhyme you out a verse about Finn and the Danish wedding.

Owen: Those old songs of Finn and his men are only for winter nights, and the feet among the sods. Give us out a new song.

Songmaker: It is best keep to the old ones. The old ones are merry, but the new ones are sorrowful.

Owen: The sorrowful songs are sometimes the best. They tell of the death of the big men and of the quarrelling of kings.

Songmaker: Well, if it is a sorrowful song you want, it is easy to find it, for there was not made these forty years any song or any story in Ireland that was not sorrowful. And if it is the quarrellings of kings you want, I will tell you of a quarrelling brought such trouble into Ireland, that if a grain of it could be blown through a pipe in amongst the angels of heaven, it would bring a dark mist over their faces. (*Rocks himself.*) I tell you, that if the half of all the tears, shed through that quarrelling, could be sent through a pipe into hell, the flames would be put out, and the hearth of it black-flooded with otters!

Owen: That must be the story of the coming of the Gall into Ireland.

Flann: That trouble is surely lessening. There are no more killings. It is best to put away old griefs out of mind. Think now of some other thing. Something happened in Spain or in France.

Dervorgilla: Do not meddle with him, Flann. It is not the telling of the story makes the story. Let me hear what is the common voice.

(*Songmaker sings:*)

It is pitiful and sharp to-day are the wounds
of Ireland,
From Galway of white flaggy stones to Cork of
the white strand;
The branches that were full of leaves and honey
on the leaves
Are torn and stripped and shortened by the
stranger to our grief.

It is long, O Royal Ireland, you were mannerly
and kind,
A nursing mother to your sons, fair, hospitable,
wise;
Now you are wine spilled from a cup beneath
the strangers' feet,
The English-speaking troop to-day have trodden
down our wheat.

The wild white fawn has lost the shape was
comely in the wood,
Since the foreign crow came nesting in the yew-
tree overhead,
Since the red East wind brought to our hurt
the troop of foreign rogues,
We are drifted like the wretched fur of a cat upon
a bog!

Flann: Where is the use of yelping and yowl-
ing like a hound that has lost the pack? Get

out of this, if that screeching of a banshee is all that you can do.

Dervorgilla: I have given him leave to sing his songs. Let him travel his own road. Let him take his own way.

Songmaker: It is hard for me to tell my story and that one not giving me leave to tell it. There must be a preparation for everything and a beginning. Would n't you hear the wind making its cry about the house before you would hear the hammering of the rain upon the stones? Give me time now, and I will give out the story of a man that has left a name will never be forgotten here, and that is Diarmuid MacMurrough, King of Leinster, that first called the English into Ireland. (*Sings:*)

Through Diarmuid's bad sway we are wasted
    to-day,
It was he brought away the Queen of Breffny;
And when O'Rourke raised Connacht against
    him,
Gave the English pay to come to Ireland.

It were better for all that are under the Gall,
If death made a call and he in the cradle;
Bind him down very strong and bruise him
    long,
The way he can wrong us no more for ever.

His great body is down under the stone
Chased by the hounds were before the world;
It was Peter's own frown closed the door before
    him,
It is Diarmuid is bound in cold Hell for ever!

Dervorgilla: That is enough, that is enough!
Why should you heap up blame upon one that
is dead? King Diarmuid's lips are closed now
with clay. It is a shameful thing, a cowardly
thing, to make attacks upon a man that cannot
answer. Are you not satisfied to let God be
the judge?

Songmaker: I had no intention to give offence.
To dispraise Diarmuid and the English, I thought
that would give satisfaction in this place, the
same as it does in Connacht.

Dervorgilla: Those that have a good heart and
a high nature try to find excuses for the dead.

Songmaker: So they would, so they would.
It is finding excuses we should be for the dead.
There is an excuse for every one; the Blessed
Mother knows that, and she sitting every Sat-
urday as the attorney for poor souls. Making
out a case for them she does be.

Dervorgilla: There is no one who might not
be freed from blame, if his case and what led to
his wrongdoing were put down.

Songmaker: I 'll make out a case for him. I

can tell out what led King Diarmuid into his sin and his treachery; and that is the thing brings mostly all mischief into the world, the changeable wagging nature of a woman. (*Sings:*)

He cares little for life, puts trust in a wife,
It is long it is known they go with the wind;
A   queer   thing a woman was   joined   with
    O'Rourke
To show herself kind to a pet from Leinster.

The rat in the larder, the fire in the thatch,
The guest to be fattening, the children famished;
If 't was Diarmuid's call that brought in the
    Gall,
Let the weight of it fall upon Dervorgilla!

> (*Dervorgilla tries to rise and cannot.   Mona
>   supports her, Flann offers her wine.
>   She lies back as if faint.   They attend
>   to her, their backs to the rest.   The singer
>   crosses to the young men, who give him
>   money.*)

Mamie: I often heard of Dervorgilla that left the King of Breffny for Diarmuid, and started the war, but I never heard what happened to her after.

Owen: There is no one knows that.   Some say King Roderick put her under locks in a cell at Clonmacnoise.

Songmaker: More likely she hanged herself, after setting the whole of the country in an uproar.

Owen: If she did they had a right to bury her with a hound on her false heart, the same as Diarmuid himself was buried.

Songmaker: No, but Diarmuid's father was buried with the hound. Excuse or no excuse, a bad race they are, a bad race.

Flann: (*To Songmaker.*) Quit off now out of this place before I will make you quit it. Take yourself and your rags and your venomous tongue out of this.

Songmaker: Let you leave me alone. Is that the way you are laying hands upon a poet?

Dervorgilla: Leave him go, Flann. You are judging him now. God is the Judge; let him go.

Songmaker: Look at the way you have me tore! It is where I 'll go on to that troop of English on the hill beyond. I 'll sound my songs for them. I will get better treatment from them itself, than I am getting from you. If it wasn't for respect for the lady, it 's a great overthrow I 'd make of you. I 'll go on to the English. (*He goes off, singing as he goes.*)

Since the Gall have the sway, it 's for them I will play
There 's none would lay blame on a boy that 's a beggar,

But a queer thing a woman was joined to
O'Rourke,
To show herself kind to a fox from Leinster!

Owen: The English look to be friendly enough.
They are drinking beer from the barrels. They
are cheering the horses that go over the bank.
Come along, boys, and see the big leaps.

Mamie: Take care now, it would not be safe
to go near the bowmen. Did n't you see the way
they made an end of that crane a while ago?

Owen: Flann said they would do no harm. I
would like well to get a near view of the big bows.
Come along, Mamie.

Mamie: I will not. I will go into the garden
of the Abbey.

> (*She goes in through gate, Owen and young
> men go out.*)

Dervorgilla: (*Raising herself up.*) Oh, my sin,
my sin has come upon my head! Why did I
come out from the Abbey walls? A cell is the
only fitting place for me! I should never have
come out into the light of the day!

Flann: Ah, what does it signify? What is
it all but a vagabond's song that was born in a
minute, and will vanish away like a wisp of smoke.

Dervorgilla: The dream of the night was true.
It is coming true. My sin is remembered — I
shall be known—I saw it all—they stooped to pick

up stones—there was no forgiveness when they knew me to be Dervorgilla!

Flann: That is a thing they will never know and that they have no way to know. Sure in the Abbey itself there is no one knows it outside the Order.

Dervorgilla: It will be discovered, some one will see me.

Flann: Ah, there are few living in any place that ever saw you in the old days. And if they should see you now itself, how would they know those holy withered cheeks to belong to the lovely lady that set kings fighting in her bloom? And many happenings have happened since then, and it is likely the Queen of Breffny is forgotten. Sure you heard them saying that Dervorgilla is dead.

Dervorgilla: I will go in. Bring me back into the shelter of the walls.

Flann: It might be best. There will be no drunken poets and schemers of the sort going in there to annoy you. It is too open-handed you are to them all, that is what makes them so stubborn and so high-minded. Gather up the pillows, Mona, till we 'll bring the lady in.

Mona: It 's best, it 's best. Ah, don't be fretting, dear. There is no one on earth knows your secret and your name but myself, that was reared with you, and this man that is my own comrade. And you know well, and I swear to you, the both of us would be dragged through briars, and ground under millstones, before we would consent to say out your name to any person at all. I would sooner my tongue to be turned to a stone here and now, than you to be uneasy the way you are.

Dervorgilla: There is no hiding it, no hiding it. Dreams come true. Who was there to-day to tell it, and that beggar told the story. He will be singing it from troop to troop. The English will hear it, the runners will hear it, it will be blazed before night through the provinces, it will set them thinking of me, and talking.

Flann: The devil skelp him! It would be no harm at all to come from behind and give him a tip of a hurl on the head to quiet his impudence and his talk. There is strength in my hand yet, and weight in my stick.

Dervorgilla: No, no, I will not have any one hurt for my sake. I will have no other blood upon my head. But follow him, Flann. Go after him and put him under bonds to go away, to leave the province, to give up his singing. Give him money, all this money, that he may live in some far-away place, without singing and wandering.

Flann: (*Taking the purse.*) I will do that. Wait three minutes and I 'll be coming back to bring you within the walls. I 'll put him under heavy oaths to quit this, to go do his croaking with the crows of Scotland. That they may make an end of him with their beaks, and be pecking the eyes out of him, and lining their nests with every hair of his head! (*He goes off.*)

Dervorgilla: It is of no use, dreams cannot lie, my punishment must come. I knew it all the time, even within the walls. I tried to make it up with good works. It was of no use, my name is in men's mouths.

Mona: What signifies one beggar's song? It is not on you the blame should be laid. It was not you went to Diarmuid MacMurrough. It was not you followed after him to Leinster. It was he came and brought you away. There are many say it was by force. There are many that are saying that. That is the way it will be written in the histories.

Dervorgilla: If Diarmuid MacMurrough had taken me by force, do you think I would have lived with him for one day only? My hands were strong then. I had my courage then. I was free to make an end of myself or of him. Will the generations think better of me, thinking me to have been taken as a prey, like the Connacht hag's basket, or the Munster hag's speckled cow? Does the marten that is torn from the woods lull itself in its master's arms?

Mona: Maybe so, maybe so. I used to be better pleased myself hearing them say it, than putting the blame on yourself of leaving O'Rourke.

Dervorgilla: O'Rourke was a good man, and a brave man, and a kinder man than Diarmuid, but it was with Diarmuid my heart was. It is to him I was promised before ever I saw O'Rourke, and I loved him better than ever my own lord, and he me also, and this was long! I loved him, I loved him! Why did they promise me to him and break the promise? Why was every one against him then and always, every one against Diarmuid? Why must they be throwing and ever-throwing sharp reproaches upon his name? Had a man loved by a king's daughter nothing in him to love? A man great of body, hardy in fight, hoarse with shouts of battle. He had liefer be dreaded than loved! It was he cast down the great, it was the dumb poor he served! Every proud man against him and he against every proud man. Oh, Diarmuid, I did not dread you. It was I myself led you astray! Let the curse and the vengeance fall upon me and me only, for the great wrong and the treachery done by both of us to Ireland!

> (*A loud cry is heard. Both look towards where it comes from.*)

Mona: Listen, listen!

Dervorgilla: What is it? What is that cry?

Mona: It is like the heavy shout does be given out over a man that has been struck down by his enemies. (*The shout is heard nearer.*)

Dervorgilla: What is it!

Mona: (*Looking out.*) The young men are coming back. Their heads are drooping.

Dervorgilla: God grant no trouble may have fallen upon them.

Mona: There is trouble, and heavy trouble upon them, sure enough.

(*Mamie comes in from garden, young men come in.*)

Dervorgilla: What is it, my children? What has happened?

Owen: The truce has been broken. The wasp we thought drowsy has found its sting. The hand of the Gall has again been reddened.

Mona: Tell it out, tell it out, what is it has happened at all?

Owen: Get ready for the burying of Flann of Breffny, the lady's steward and distributor, and your good comrade.

Mona: Ah! that is foolishness. It cannot be true. He was here but a minute ago, standing in this spot.

Owen: It is true.

Dervorgilla: How did he die? Tell me all.

Owen: He came where that Connachtman was doing his tricks for the English troop. They asked a song of him; he was going to give it

out. Flann tried to bring him away. The bowmen had mugs of beer in their hands; they were
laughing at the tricks; they wanted the song.
They called out to Flann to leave him to make
fun for them, but Flann tried to bring him
away. He spoke in his ear; he put his hand
over his mouth. They were rightly vexed then,
and one of them called out: "There, spoil-sport,
is a spoiling of all sport for you," and he drew
his bow and sent an arrow through Flann's body,
that he fell like a stone, without a word. Then
they turned their horses, and one of them said it was
a pity, but another said their dinners would be spoiling in Drogheda. And so they rode away in a hurry.

Dervorgilla: Another. Death has come upon
another. (*Holds out her hands.*) Come to me,
my poor Mona, my friend.

Mona: Is it Flann is dead? Flann, my husband? He had a year less than I myself had.
It was not his time to die. Who is there to
close my own eyes now? He always said he
would close my eyes.

Dervorgilla: Your trouble is no greater than
my trouble. It was for my sake and in following
my bidding he died.

Mona: It was the Gall killed his two brothers
and destroyed the house and trampled down the
field of oats. What did they want killing
him? Wasn't it enough to have destroyed his oats?

Dervorgilla: Come into the Abbey and prepare for him there.

Mona: So near to the chapel, and not a priest to overtake him before he died. That was no death for a Christian man.

Dervorgilla: Candles will be lighted, and many Masses said for his soul.

Mona: And if it was with the sword itself he was killed, that 's natural. His brothers were killed with the sword. But an arrow! Not one of the family was killed with that before. That is not a thing you would be hearing in the ballads.

Owen: Will you go where the body is? There are some that are laying it out?

Mona: I will, I will. Bring me to my decent comrade; and bring me to that singer was here. I will lay it upon him to make a great cursing to put upon the Gall, a great heavy curse upon all that had to do with the Gall. (*She is going off, but turns back to Dervorgilla.*) But it is not on yourself I will let them put a curse, or lay on you any blame at all. You know well I never put blame on you, or said a sharp word of you, the time you were in Breffny with O'Rourke, or the time you were in Leinster with Diarmuid MacMurrough, and I myself following you from place to place. You know well, and the man that is stretched cold and dumb knows, I never said a hard word or an unkind word or a bad word of you yourself, Dervorgilla. (*She goes out babbling.*) Oh, no, no; I would never do such a thing as that!

Owen: (*To the others.*) Dervorgilla! Oh, did you hear her say it is Dervorgilla?

Dervorgilla: (*Stands up with difficulty.*) Since you were born and before you were born I have been here, kneeling and praying, kneeling and praying, fasting and asking forgiveness of God. I think my father God has forgiven me. They tell me my mother the Church has forgiven me. That old man had forgiven me, and he had suffered by the Gall. The old—the old—that old woman, even in her grief, she called out no word against me. You are young. You will surely forgive me, for you are young. (*They are all silent. Then Owen comes over and lays down his cup at her feet, then turns and walks slowly away.*) It is not your hand has done this, but the righteous hand of God that has moved your hand. (*Other lads lay down their gifts.*) I take this shame for the shame in the west I put on O'Rourke of Breffny, and the death I brought upon him by the hand of the Gall. (*The youngest boy, who has hesitated, comes and lays down his hurl and silver ball, and goes away, his head drooping.*) I take this reproach for the reproach in the east I brought upon Diarmuid, King of Leinster, thrusting upon him wars and attacks and battles, till for his defence and to defend Leinster, he called in the strangers that have devoured Ireland. (*The young men have all gone. Mamie comes as if to lay down her gift, but draws back. Dervorgilla turns to her.*) Do not be afraid to give back my gifts, do not separate yourself from your companions for my sake. For there is little of my life but is spent, and there has come upon me this day all the pain of the world and its anguish, seeing and knowing that a deed once done has no undoing, and the lasting trouble my unfaithfulness has brought upon you and your children for ever. (*Mamie lays down her necklace and goes away sadly.*) There is kindness in your unkindness, not leaving me to go and face Michael and the Scales of Judgment wrapped in comfortable words, and the praises of the poor, and the lulling of psalms, but from the swift, unflinching, terrible judgment of the young! (*She sinks slowly to the ground holding to the chair. The stage begins to darken; the voice of the Songmaker is heard coming nearer, singing:*)

The rat in the cupboard, the fire in the lap;
The guest to be fattening, the children fretting;
My curse upon all that brought in the Gall,
Upon Diarmuid's call, and on Dervorgilla!

Curtain

MUSIC FOR THE
SONGS IN THE PLAYS
NOTES AND CASTS

MUSIC FOR DERVORGILLA

Yesterday travelling Connacht, Drogheda has me to-
day, My back to the emp - ty pock- ets... My
face to the place will pay! Just rov-ing a-
round To my grief and my sor - row,
Un - der a rock to-day, Un - der a bush to-
mor - row... Sy - rup- y sweet to - day,
Sour as sloes to -mor- row; Sweet to the lads that
pay, Sour to the lads that bor - row!

1. I am after being   given two grand steppers
2. It's the roads of the world would be proud to see them,

Matching one another   like two swallows on the   wind,
It's a great ornament   they will be, far and   near;

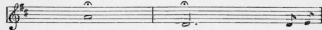

Made from the skin of the Brown Bull of Cuailgne, Or the
She that gave them never learned to be a niggard, Tho' the

cow Ar - gus-mind - ed, ...   he that was not blind.
Gall are a - mong us this four and twenty year !

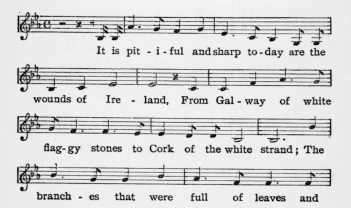

It is pit - i - ful and sharp to - day are the

wounds of   Ire - land, From Gal - way of white

flag - gy stones to Cork of the white strand; The

branch - es that were full   of leaves and

hon - ey on the leaves Are torn and stripped and
short - ened by the stranger to our grief. It is
long, O Royal Ire - land, you were manner - ly and
kind, A nurs - ing mo - ther to your sons, fair,
hos - pi - ta - ble, wise; Now you are wine spilled
from a cup be-neath the stran-gers' feet, The
English-speaking troop to-day have trod-den down our wheat.

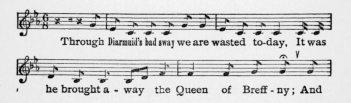

Through Diarmuid's bad sway we are wasted to-day, It was
he brought a - way the Queen of Breff - ny; And

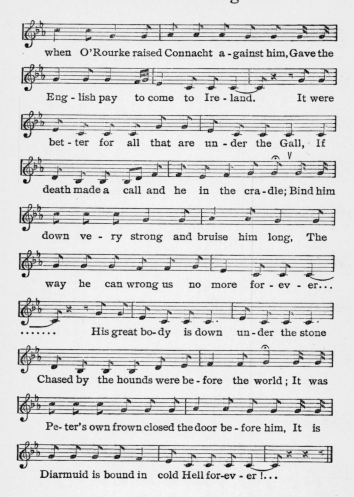

when O'Rourke raised Connacht a - gainst him, Gave the

Eng - lish pay to come to Ire - land. It were

bet - ter for all that are un - der the Gall, If

death made a call and he in the cra - dle; Bind him

down ve - ry strong and bruise him long, The

way he can wrong us no more for - ev - er...

.... His great bo - dy is down un - der the stone

Chased by the hounds were be - fore the world; It was

Pe - ter's own frown closed the door be - fore him, It is

Diarmuid is bound in cold Hell for-ev - er !...

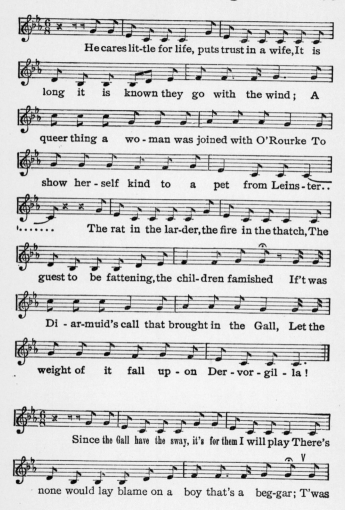

He cares lit-tle for life, puts trust in a wife, It is
long it is known they go with the wind; A
queer thing a wo - man was joined with O'Rourke To
show her - self kind to a pet from Leins - ter..
.... The rat in the lar-der, the fire in the thatch, The
guest to be fattening, the chil-dren famished If 't was
Di - ar-muid's call that brought in the Gall, Let the
weight of it fall up - on Der - vor - gil - la !

Since the Gall have the sway, it's for them I will play There's
none would lay blame on a boy that's a beg-gar; T'was

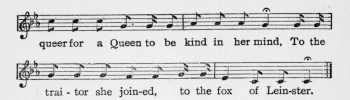

queer for   a Queen to be kind in her mind, To the

trai - tor she join-ed,   to the fox   of Lein-ster.

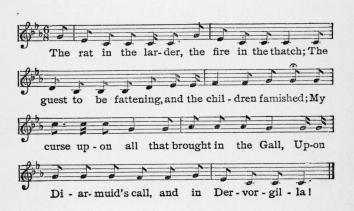

The rat in the lar-der, the fire in the thatch; The

guest to   be fattening, and the chil - dren famished; My

curse up-on   all that brought in   the Gall, Up-on

Di - ar- muid's call, and   in Der - vor - gil - la!

NOTES

GRANIA

I THINK I turned to Grania because so many have
written about sad, lovely Deirdre, who when overtaken
by sorrow made no good battle at the last. Grania
had more power of will, and for good or evil twice took
the shaping of her life into her own hands. The riddle
she asks us through the ages is, "Why did I, having left
great grey-haired Finn for comely Diarmuid, turn back
to Finn in the end, when he had consented to Diarmuid's death?" And a question tempts one more
than the beaten path of authorised history. If I
have held but lightly to the legend, it is not because
I do not know it, for in *Gods and Fighting Men* I have
put together and rejected many versions. For the
present play I have taken but enough of the fable on
which to set, as on a sod of grass, the three lovers, one
of whom had to die. I suppose it is that "fascina-
tion of things difficult" that has tempted me to write
a three-act play with only three characters. Yet
where Love itself, with its shadow Jealousy, is the
true protagonist I could not feel that more were
needed. When I told Mr. Yeats I had but these
three persons in the play, he said incredulously,

"They must have a great deal to talk about." And so they have, for the talk of lovers is inexhaustible, being of themselves and one another.

As to the Fianna, the Fenians, I have heard their story many a time from my neighbours, old men who have drifted into workhouses, seaweed gatherers on the Burren Coast, turf-cutters on Slieve Echtge, and the like. For though the tales that have gathered around that mysterious race are thought by many to come from the earliest days, even before the coming of the Aryan Celt, the people of the West have a very long memory. And these tales are far better remembered than those of the Red Branch, and this, it is suggested, is part proof of their having belonged to the aboriginal race. Cuchulain's bravery, and Deirdre's beauty "that brought the Sons of Usnach to their death" find their way, indeed, into the folk-poetry of all the provinces; but the characters of the Fianna, Grania's fickleness, and Conan's bitter tongue, and Oisin's gentleness to his friends and his keen wit in the arguments with St. Patrick, and Goll's strength, and Osgar's high bravery, and Finn's wisdom, that was beyond that of earth, are as well known as the characteristics of any noticeable man of modern times.

An old man I talked with on the beach beyond Kinvara told me, "They were very strong in those days, and six or seven feet high. I was digging the potato garden one day about forty years ago, and down in the dyke the spade struck against something, and it was the bones of a man's foot, and it was three feet long. I brought away one bone of it myself, and the man that was along with me, but we buried it after. It was the foot of one of those men. They had every one six or seven dogs, and first they would set two of the dogs to fight, and then they'd fight themselves. And they'd go to all countries in curraghs that were as strong as steamers; to Spain they went in their curraghs. They went across from this hill of Burren to Connemara one time, and the sea opened to let them pass. There are no men like them now; the Connemara men are the best, but even with them, if there was a crowd of them together, and you to throw a stick over their heads, it would hardly hit one, they are mostly all the one height, and no one a few inches taller than another."

Another man says, "They were all strong men in those times; and one time Finn and his men went over to Granagh to fight the men there, and it was the time of the harvest, and what they fought with was sheaves, and every one that got a blow of a sheaf got his death. There is one of them buried now in Fardy Whelan's hill, and there's two headstones, and my father often measured the grave, and he said it is seven yards long."

On Slieve Echtge I was told, "Oisin and Finn took the lead for strength, and Samson, too, he had great strength." "I would rather hear about the Irish strong men," said I. "Well, and Samson was of the Irish race, all the world was Irish in those times, and he killed the Philistines, and the eyes were picked out of him after. He was said to be the strongest, but I think myself Finn MacCumhail was stronger."

And again, "It was before the flood those strong men lived here, Finn and Oisin and the others, and they lived longer than people do now, three or four hundred years.

"Giants they were; Conan was twelve feet high, and he was the smallest. But ever since, people are getting smaller and smaller, and will till they come to the end; but they are wittier and more crafty than they were in the old days, for the giants were innocent though they were so strong."

I hear sometimes of "a small race and dark, and that carried the bag," and that was probably the aboriginal one. "There was a low-sized race came, that worked the land of Ireland a long time; they had their time like the others." And, "Finn was the last of the giants, the tall strong men. It was after that the Lochlannachs came to the country. They were very small, but they were more crafty than the giants, and they used to be humbugging them. One time they got a sack and filled it with sand, and gave it to one of the Fianna to put on his back to try him. But he lifted it up, and all he said was, 'It is grain sowed in February it is.'" Another says, "An old man that was mending the wall of the house used to be telling stories about the strong men of the old time; very small they were, about three feet high, but they were very strong for all that."

Grania is often spoken of as belonging to that small race, as if her story had come from a very early time. "She was very small, only four feet. She was the heiress of the princes of Ireland, and that is why they were after her." "They say Diarmuid and Grania were very small. They made the big cromlechs, there's a slab on the one near Crusheen, sixteen men could n't lift, but they had *their own way* of doing it." And again, "Diarmuid and Grania were very small and very thick." Another says, "Grania was low-sized; and people now are handsomer than the people of the old time, but they have n't such good talk."

I do not know if it is because of Grania's breach of faith, that I never hear her spoken of with sympathy, and her name does not come into the songs as Deirdre's does. A blind piper told me, "Some say Grania was handsome, and some say she was ugly, there's a saying in Irish for that." And an old basket-maker was scornful and said, "Many would tell you Grania slept under the cromlechs, but I don't believe that, and she a king's daughter. And I don't believe she was handsome either. If she was, why would she have run away?"

An old woman says, "Finn had more wisdom than all the men in the world, but he was n't wise enough to put a bar on Grania. It was huts with big stones Grania made, that are called cromlechs now; they made them when they went away into the wilderness."

And again I was told at Moycullen, near Lough Corrib, "As they were passing a stream, the water splashed on Grania, and she said 'Diarmuid was never so near to me as that.'"

KINCORA

Kincora was the first historical play I wrote, and

it gave me a great deal of trouble and I wrote many versions, for I had not enough of skill to wrestle with the mass of material, and I think I kept too closely to history. It was produced at the Abbey Theatre in 1905 in the old printed version. This new version was produced in 1909.

I hoped then and still hope that we may give a week or more in every year to a sequence of history plays, or perhaps play them at schools, that schoolboys and schoolgirls may have their imagination stirred about the people who made history, instead of knowing them but as names. But Brian's greatness lives always in the memory of the people, and Kincora is remembered in the song translated by Mangan from the Irish of one of Brian's own household:

Oh, where, Kincora, is Brian the great? And where is
the beauty that once was thine?
Oh, where are the princes and nobles that sat at the
feast in thy halls and drank the red wine?

. . . .

I am MacLiag and my home is on the lake; thither
often to that palace whose beauty is dead
Came Brian to ask me and I went for his sake. Oh my
grief! that I should live and Brian be dead!

The summary given by modern histories is as follows:

"Two Kings gained lasting renown during the contests with the Norsemen, Malachi the Great, who became High King in 980, and Brian, King of the province of Munster. Brian in a battle fought in 968

at Sulcoit, north of the Galtee Mountains, defeated
the Norsemen and put them to flight.   This was the
first of a series of victories against the raiders who
from this time forward are generally spoken of as
Danes, though they came from Norway as well as
Denmark.

"Malachi, the High King, was at the same time making attacks on the invaders' settlements in Dublin and
as far north as the Boyne.   He took Dublin in 996,
winning there among other spoils the golden ring of
a Danish chief.   Two such strong personalities as
Malachi and Brian, rulers of provinces which had long
been rivals, could hardly be expected to live in
brotherly union and concord.   We find them constantly
at strife, even when both were fighting against the
common foe.   They finally agreed to divide Ireland
between them, Malachi taking the northern part and
handing over the southern to Brian.   This arrange-
ment was made in 998, and not unnaturally gave great
offence to the King of Leinster whose territory lay in
the region assigned by Malachi to Brian.   The King
of Leinster made an alliance with the Danes of Dublin
and determined to resist Brian's authority.   Brian and
Malachi immediately gathered an army and met and
defeated the united armies of the King of Leinster and
the Danes in one of the valleys of the Wicklow hills,
Glenmama.

"Brian married Gormleith (Gormley), sister of the
King of Leinster and widow of a former chief of the
Danes, whose son Sitric was now their acknowledged
leader.   This alliance won over to Brian's side both the

King of Leinster and the Danes of Dublin, and Brian presently felt strong enough to lead an army northward towards Tara to try conclusions with Malachi for the High Kingship of Ireland. Malachi recognised that his opponent was too strong for him and made his submission. This took place in the year 1002, and for the next twelve years, until he was slain at the battle of Clontarf, Brian was recognised as the High King of Ireland."

That is what the histories tell, and they tell also of the woman who walked all Ireland with a gold ring in her hand; though I have changed the rich clothes of the legend for rags, thinking them nearer to the inner meaning of the parable. As to the quarrel between Brian and the King of Leinster, the books say:

"As part of his tribute the Leinster King was bringing to Kincora three pine trees for ships' masts, and among the carriers some dispute arose as to who was to be in the first place. To end the dispute the King himself took the first place, and in his exertions in carrying the tree, one of the silver buttons of his tunic had been torn off. At Kincora he handed the tunic to his sister Gormleith, asking her to sew on the displaced button; but the lady, instead, heaped reproaches on him for being a mere vassal, and angrily flung the tunic into the fire. Her taunting words irritated Maelmora, and his irritation was soon shown. Looking on at a game of chess which was being played between Murrough and his cousin Conaing, Maelmora suggested a move which ended in Murrough losing the

game. Murrough angrily remarked, 'That was like
the advice you gave the Danes which lost them Glenmama.' Maelmora with equal anger replied, 'I will
now give them advice and they shall not be defeated.'
'Then' said Murrough, 'you had better remind them
to have a yew tree ready for your reception.' For
Maelmora had hidden in a yew tree after his defeat at
Glenmama. In bitterness of heart and in secret
Maelmora left Kincora. He decided to revolt and
was joined by the Dublin Danes. The battle of
Clontarf was the result. Brian was killed there,
and Maelmora, but the Danes were driven from Ireland
for ever.

"In bringing together the Danes for Clontarf
nobody had been more active than Gormleith. Since
Maelmora's visit to Kincora she had been repudiated
by Brian and had become so 'grim' against him that
she wished him dead. She had sent her son Sitric
to the Danish leaders to beg their assistance. The
two best known of these leaders were Brodar, Earl of
Man, and Sigurd, Earl of Orkney. Both made it a
condition to be acknowledged King of Ireland if Brian
were defeated and slain, and also to get Gormleith in
marriage . . . though the latter was now old, and it is
unlikely that they were attracted by her doubtful
virtue or coveted her faded charms."

So far the histories, founded, one must think, on the
legends of the people. Around Kincora such legends
still linger. One is shown where Brian's palace was,
and where the fish were caught for his use, and told of

all his cellars and strong-rooms and passages, some of
them underground. And a man in armour is seen
now and again on the roads near the green mound
where the palace stood, who is, it may be, the walking
shadow of the High King.

When *Kincora* was first produced in Dublin, an old
farmer came all the way from Killaloe near Kincora
to see it, and he went away sad because as he said
" Brian ought not to have married that woman, but to
have been content with a nice quiet girl from his own
district."

As to the Danes, the people tell me, "The reason of
the wisps and the fires on Saint John's Eve is that one
time long ago the Danes came and took the country
and conquered it, and they put a soldier to mind every
house through the whole country. And at last the
people made up their minds that on one night they
would kill the soldiers. So they did as they said, and
there wasn't one left, and that is why they light the
wisps ever since. It was Brian Boroihme (Boru) was
the first to light them. There was not much of an army
left to the Danes that time, for he made a great scatter
of them. A great man he was, and his own son was
as good, that is Murrough. It was the wife brought
him to his end, Gormleith. She was for war, and he
was all for peace. And he got to be very pious, too
pious, and old, and she got tired of that." And I am
told of the last battle. "Clontarf was on the head
of a game of chess. The generals of the Danes were
beaten at it, and they were vexed. It was Brodar,

that the Brodericks are descended from, that put a dagger through Brian's heart, and he attending to his prayers. What the Danes left in Ireland were hens and weasels. And when the cock crows in the morning the country people will always say, 'It is for Denmark they are crowing; crowing they are to be back in Denmark.'"

But the Danes are often mixed up with the Tuatha de Danaan, the old gods, the invisible inhabitants of the forths, as in a story I have been told of the battle of Aughrim. "The Danes were dancing in the forths around Aughrim the night after the battle. Their ancestors were driven out of Ireland before; and they were glad when they saw those that had put them out put out themselves, and every one of them skivered."

The small size of our stage and our small number of players forced me to do away with what our people call "the middling class," and I have used but servants and kings. As to their language, I have, to the grief of my printers, used the dialect spoken by many of my neighbours, who are though it may be by long descent, belonging to the families of kings.

DERVORGILLA

Dervorgilla, daughter of the King of Meath, wife of O'Rourke, King of Breffny, was taken away, willingly or unwillingly, by Diarmuid MacMurrough, King of Leinster, in the year 1152. O'Rourke and his friends invaded Leinster in revenge, and in the wars which followed, Diarmuid, driven from Ireland, appealed for help to Henry II of England, and was given an army under Strongbow, to whom Diarmuid promised Leinster as reward. It is so the English were first brought into Ireland. Dervorgilla, having outlived O'Rourke and Diarmuid and Henry and Strongbow, is said to have died at the Abbey of Mellifont, near Drogheda, in the year 1193, aged 85.

That is how the story is told in the histories. And I have heard in Kiltartan: " Dervorgilla was a red-haired woman, and it was she put the great curse on Ireland, bringing in the English through Mac-Murrough, that she went to from O'Rourke. It was to Henry the Second MacMurrough went, and he sent Strongbow, and they stopped in Ireland ever since. But who knows but another race might be worse, such as the Spaniards that were scattered along the whole coast of Connacht at the time of the Armada? And the laws are good enough. I heard it said the English will be dug out of their graves one day for the sake of their law. As to Dervorgilla, she was not brought away by force, she went to MacMurrough herself. For there are men in the world that have a coaxing way, and sometimes women are weak."

Dates and casts of the first production of these plays at the Abbey Theatre, Dublin.

GRANIA has not yet been produced.

KINCORA. This revised version of KINCORA was produced February 11, 1909, with the following cast:

Brian	ARTHUR SINCLAIR
Maelmora	SYDNEY J. MORGAN
Malachi	AMBROSE POWER
Sitric	U. WRIGHT
Murrough	FRED O'DONOVAN
Brennain	J. M. KERRIGAN
Rury	J. H. DUNNE
Phelan	J. A. O'ROURKE
Gormleith	SARA ALLGOOD
Beggar	MAIRE O'NEILL

DERVORGILLA was produced October 31, 1907, with the following cast:

Dervorgilla	SARA ALLGOOD
Mona	MAIRE O'NEILL
Mamie.	BRIGIT O'DEMPSEY
Flann	F. J. FAY
Songmaker	W. G. FAY
A Boy	ARTHUR SINCLAIR
Another	J. M. KERRIGAN
Another	J. A. O'ROURKE

Irish Plays

By
LADY GREGORY

Lady Gregory's name has become a household word in America and her works should occupy an exclusive niche in every library. Mr. George Bernard Shaw, in a recently published interview, said Lady Gregory "is the greatest living Irishwoman. . . . Even in the plays of Lady Gregory, penetrated as they are by that intense love of Ireland which is unintelligible to the many drunken blackguards with Irish names who make their nationality an excuse for their vices and their worthlessness, there is no flattery of the Irish; she writes about the Irish as Molière wrote about the French, having a talent curiously like Molière."

"The witchery of Yeats, the vivid imagination of Synge, the amusing literalism mixed with the pronounced romance of their imitators, have their place and have been given their praise without stint. But none of these can compete with Lady Gregory for the quality of universality. The best beauty in Lady Gregory's art is its spontaneity. It is never forced. . . . She has read and dreamed and studied, and slept and wakened and worked, and the great ideas that have come to her have been nourished and trained till they have grown to be of great stature."—*Chicago Tribune.*

G. P. PUTNAM'S SONS
NEW YORK   **LONDON**

DATE DUE

GAYLORD			PRINTED IN U S A